COACHING SWIMMING SUCCESSFULLY

Dick Hannula

Tacoma Swim Club, Tacoma, WA

Human Kinetics

Library of Congress Cataloging-in-Publication Data

Hannula, Dick, 1928-
    Coaching swimming successfully / Dick Hannula.
        p.   cm.
    Includes index.
    ISBN 0-87322-492-2
    1. Swimming--Coaching.   I. Title.
    GV837.65.H35   1995   94-10232
    797.2'1--dc20   CIP

ISBN: 0-87322-492-2

Developmental Editor: Mary E. Fowler
Assistant Editors: Anna Curry and Hank Woolsey
Copyeditor: Anthony Brown
Proofreader: Kathy Bennett
Indexer: Sheila Ary
Typesetters: Sonnie Bowman and Kathy Boudreau-Fuoss
Text Designer: Keith Blomberg
Layout Artists: Denise Lowry, Tara Welsch, and Kathy Boudreau-Fuoss
Cover Photo: John Kelly
Illustrator: Accurate Art, Inc.
Printer: Sheridan Press

Copies of this book are available at special discounts for bulk purchase for sales promotions, premiums, fund-raising, or educational use. Special editions or book excerpts can also be created to specifications. For details, contact the Special Sales Manager at Human Kinetics.

Printed in the United States of America   10   9   8   7   6   5

Human Kinetics
Web site: http://www.humankinetics.com/

United States: Human Kinetics, P.O. Box 5076, Champaign, IL 61825-5076
1-800-747-4457
e-mail: humank@hkusa.com

Canada: Human Kinetics, 475 Devonshire Road, Unit 100, Windsor, ON N8Y 2L5
1-800-465-7301 (in Canada only)
e-mail: humank@hkcanada.com

Europe: Human Kinetics, P.O. Box IW14, Leeds LS16 6TR, United Kingdom
(44) 1132 781708
e-mail: humank@hkeurope.com

Australia: Human Kinetics, 57A Price Avenue, Lower Mitcham, South Australia 5062
(088) 277 1555
e-mail: humank@hkaustralia.com

New Zealand: Human Kinetics, P.O. Box 105-231, Auckland 1
(09) 523 3462
e-mail: humank@hknewz.com

To my wife, Sylvia; our children, Dan, Dave, Dick, and Debby; our grandchildren; and my mother, Katherine.

Contents

Foreword

When it comes to coaching swimming, Dick Hannula is without peer. His record speaks for itself: 24 consecutive boys' high school state championships; a career high school winning percentage of nearly 95%; being founder and head coach of the Tacoma Swim Club; preparing swimmers to earn positions on Olympic, Pan Am, and World Championship teams. One of his best swimmers was Kaye Hall, a member of the Tacoma Swim Club, who went on to win two Olympic gold medals and one bronze.

Dick's success as a coach, however, is even more evident in how he handles the intangibles that have let him achieve such a great record over his 40-plus years of coaching. His enthusiasm for learning about the new science and technology of swimming, his ability to teach swimmers the information he gathers, his motivation of athletes through positive reinforcement rather than punishment, his development of good people as well as good athletes—these are the qualities that truly set Dick apart.

In this book, Dick leaves no stone unturned. He explains the importance and process of developing a coaching philosophy and communicating it, how to plan for practices, how to teach technical stroke information, how to prepare for and coach at meets, and how to evaluate swimmers and an overall program.

With *Coaching Swimming Successfully*, coaches at all levels can benefit from one of the greatest coaches our sport has ever known. Anyone, including swimmers and their parents, who reads it will not only learn more about swimming but will appreciate the role swimming can play in their lives.

I encourage you to read and learn from this valuable book. It's a great source of information and insight for coaches and their swimmers. I'll refer to it often, and I'll be a better coach for having read it.

Skip Kenney
Stanford University

Acknowledgments

Thanks to the American Swimming Coaches' Association, the National Interscholastic Swimming Coaches' Association, and United States Swimming for the many educational and professional experiences that prepared me to write this book. I also thank the many coaches that have shared their time and talent with me to make me a better coach; every swimmer who ever swam for me—your efforts and commitment have made my coaching experience exciting and rewarding; the school administrators and parents who have allowed me the freedom to be myself and coach my way; and, finally, my wife Sylvia, who has always encouraged me in my coaching and who has been my reviewer and helpful critic during the writing of this book.

Introduction

I became a head coach in 1951, when little information was available about the science or art of coaching swimming. So I struggled and learned by experience. Now we have extensive swimming research that provides a wealth of information about the scientific aspects of our sport: training programs, stroke mechanics, fluid dynamics, and so on. In this book, I share with you how the latest scientific principles can be incorporated into your swim instruction.

But in *Coaching Swimming Successfully* I emphasize the art—not the science—of coaching. You'll find good, practical advice: the kind of advice you can relate to and apply directly to your situation, that comes from having spent 40-some years of my life coaching swimmers.

My reason for writing *Coaching Swimming Successfully* is to help you accelerate and improve your coaching education—to make you a better swim coach *now*. I hope that after reading the book you will be more equipped to offer a program that provides each swimmer a positive, exciting, and rewarding experience. *Coaching Swimming Successfully* shows you how to challenge your swimmers to become better team members and to get their best swimming results. With your help, every swimmer can have a better understanding of his or her role in becoming the best swimmer that he or she can be.

We all know that swimming can be a routine, isolated sport. Practice sessions can be long and they may not offer much excitement or variety. It's hard to have interaction with your swimmers when their faces are in the water. But swimming need not be boring. In *Coaching Swimming Successfully*, I'll explain how you can

- make your swimmers excited about each training session,
- instill pride and the love of swimming in your athletes, and
- help your swimmers get the most from themselves and still have fun.

We have a great opportunity in swimming to help develop strong, motivated, capable individuals who can be leaders in all walks of life. Winning, in the pool and in life, is not always being Number 1. Winning is being the best you can be, measuring yourself against yourself, and striving to improve. We are in a position to help our swimmers and their parents understand what success really means.

For me, the job of a swim coach is a job in name only. As you read this book, you'll see that I love practices, love the thrill of competitions, and won't ever consider what I do a job. Here's hoping that *Coaching Swimming Successfully* will make you feel as good or even better than I do about being a swim coach!

Part I

Coaching
Foundation

Chapter 1

Developing a Swimming Coaching Philosophy

My coaching philosophy has a simple foundation: The most important people to me, after my family, are the athletes that I see and coach almost daily. I care about all of the swimmers on our team, whether they are the fastest or the slowest. The faces may change each year, but my philosophy remains the same.

A swimming coach's success is measured by the progress and the development of the swimmers. Although you may have a limited talent pool to draw from, the athletes who do make up your team should reflect the teaching, the training, and the discipline you've given them. This reflection is made visible by their actions in and out of the pool.

In this chapter I'll present the principles that form the foundation of my philosophy, and I'll describe how I share that philosophy through the goals I establish for my swimming program. Remember that my philosophy influences all phases of my coaching, just as your outlook affects your actions.

Every coach must determine his or her own philosophy—the unwavering principles that will provide consistency and clarity in decision making. All of the most successful coaches in our sport, from Peter Daland, George Haines, and Doc Counsilman to Mark Schubert, Skip Kenney, and Richard Quick, have demonstrated the importance of leading a swimming program with a steady and clear vision.

Origin of a Philosophy

Your philosophy of coaching is developed from your own experiences, both in swimming and in life. Experiences specific to your swimming coaching philosophy would include these:

- Books and magazine articles you have read
- Videos you have watched
- Clinics you have attended
- Experiences you have had as a swimmer and a swim coach
- Conversations you have had with athletes and coaching colleagues
- Observations you have made of other coaches at training or competitions

Many coaches have had the invaluable opportunity to intern with an experienced and successful coach. I have had many young coaches intern with me, for periods ranging from 2 weeks to 9 months. Other coaches have told me about spending a week or more just watching the training sessions of a successful coach. Even veteran coaches like me can learn by watching successful coaches train swimmers their way in their own pool.

A WEEKEND VISIT

I remember one weekend in 1984 when I talked my wife, Sylvia, into a trip to Portland, Oregon, where I wanted to watch a training session at the Multnomah Athletic Club. Skip Runkle, though young, was already a very successful coach, and some of his swimmers were ranked nationally in the individual medley. In my Saturday morning visit I learned Skip's cycle method of training, covering all four swimming strokes on different days in pulling, kicking, sprinting, distance, and stroke drills. Skip willingly shared this and more with me, and I came away from the visit a better coach.

Another major opportunity to watch successful coaches is at the national championships. At the first national championship meets I attended, I had the opportunity to watch great coaches and swimmers in action.

At my first national championship I watched the coach and his world record holder in the backstroke in the warm-up pool. They used drills to improve technique at the championship meet. I catalogued those drills for extensive use when I would be able to use them with my swimmers in our training sessions. These drills were new to me and proved very successful for my backstroke swimmers the next season.

Such learning opportunities are all around you, so take advantage of them when they present themselves. I have never found a successful swim coach who wasn't willing to share ideas.

All of your experiences with other coaches will factor into the development of your philosophical base. I would encourage you to keep adding to that base through your contacts with the many excellent former and active swim coaches available to you.

Defining Your Philosophy

Every coach must develop a philosophy that will be the base for coaching decisions. My philosophy grew from three key sources. One was Coach Howard Firby of Canada, who was the greatest teacher of stroke fundamentals that I've known. He impressed on me the need to teach technique effectively to achieve any success as a swim coach.

Another source was Coach John Tallman, formerly of the University of Washington. John was a scientist long before science entered into swim coaching. Always challenging and forming new ideas, John made me aware and appreciative of changes in coaching.

The third source was my friend Bob Miller, who coached in Seattle and more recently in Bellevue, Washington. Bob, himself an athlete, had the ability to train hard and to challenge his swimmers accordingly. Through him I learned to better appreciate the value of hard work in swimming success.

After more than 40 years of coaching swimming, I have developed six equally important tenets for my philosophy. (You may add or subtract from these in defining your own philosophy.)

1. ***There is no substitute for hard work.*** All swimmers must invest their time and effort into the sport. Success in competition is the direct result of how much work each individual puts into it. Similarly, there are no shortcuts for a coach. Consistent and persistent effort by athletes and coaches is a prerequisite for achieving anything worthwhile in swimming.

2. ***Every athlete counts.*** A team is only as strong as its weakest link. You

must be concerned about the attitude and the improvement of every team member. Team strength comes from raising the standards of all team members.

3. ***Winning is not just being Number One.*** Every swimmer on your team can be and should be a winner. A winner sets goals and then strives to attain them. Both swimmers and coaches who *continue* to strive for their goals are winners. Winning must be measured against one meaningful and reliable standard—yourself. As the coach, you have to accept this philosophy of winning and have to educate your swimmers and their parents on it.

4. ***Responsibility is required.*** The greatest power you have is the ability to choose. However, your choices require responsibility. Because you choose to coach, you are responsible for your team's results. Similarly, because your swimmers choose to be on the team, they must accept the responsibilities of their choice.

A MATTER OF CHOICE

Your swimmers can choose to study for an exam or to watch television during their available study time. While in training, your swimmers can choose to get the necessary sleep each night or they can decide to stay up late and report to practice tired. In each case the swimmers must bear the responsibility for the choices they make.

5. ***Teach first and train second.*** Keep returning to basics. All swimmers must establish good technique before they can train effectively.

6. ***Change is necessary.*** In coaching, change is a fact of life. The athletes you work with and the "best" ways to teach and to train them will change. Such variations are sometimes necessary for your own motivation.

A CHANGE ISN'T ALWAYS FOREVER

One very successful year, our team used a method of cycle training that was the result of a college class on "Physiology and the Swimming Coach." The following year we intended to follow the same precise procedure, but after the first week I called my team together and told them I couldn't get excited about the same program again this year. We all agreed and had a more successful year because of the meaningful changes made in the program.

One key to longevity in coaching is adapting to change. Programs need to be dynamic to maintain the enthusiasm of the athletes and the coach.

Be Comfortable and Be Yourself

Though your philosophy may change somewhat over your years of coaching, the core of your philosophy—those tenets that revolve around your value system and that comprise what you want your swimmers to receive from your program—probably won't change. In order for your basic philosophy to be comfortable, it will have to conform to your value system.

You need to be yourself, so don't adopt a philosophy that isn't you. Be the best that you can be and do it your way. Each coach will have his or her own style of teaching, communicating, and motivating swimmers. Copying some other coach's style won't necessarily work best for you. You have your own unique style, so develop it and make it the best for you.

Stay Hungry

You will never learn all there is to learn about coaching swimming. Be eager to learn throughout your coaching career, because the coach who thinks that she or he knows it all is on a downhill slide. Learning opportunities are all around you, so learn to recognize and to use them.

Go a Step Beyond

We have the opportunity to be a strong and positive influence on the young people we coach. We can't betray the great amount of trust they place in us. We must never lose sight of the great impact that we have on our athletes' lives. Beyond developing their technical and competitive skills, we, as coaches, have a responsibility to our athletes.

It gives coaches a great satisfaction to have their former swimmers keep in touch throughout their lives. An invitation to a wedding or to a college graduation (in my case it is often for one of my swimmers' children) reminds you of your responsibility to make the swimming experience a very positive one in your swimmers' lives.

Equal Opportunity, Not Equal Time

In college I wrote a paper on coaching swimming and said I would always give the same amount of time to each athlete. I gave a lengthy, albeit naive, explanation of how I would divide practice time evenly among team members.

However, over the years I have discovered that it is impractical to give equal time to each athlete, because they all have different needs. There is no time allotment that can be prescribed across the board.

What I have found to be more important and practical than giving equal time is giving each athlete equal opportunity to take advantage of my desire to work with all of them. Those who are willing to give more of themselves in training and competition gain the most benefit from my coaching efforts.

Important Beliefs

I am not suggesting that you adopt my coaching principles—you must feel comfortable with and committed to your own set of beliefs—but what I am recommending is that you recognize how critical your beliefs are to your coaching. On a daily basis you will be selling your athletes on the things you believe in, and like most coaches and athletes, you believe in those things that you have seen work. The more you see something succeed, the more confident you become—the stronger your belief—that it will succeed again.

As coach you must develop a philosophy, teaching method, and training program that you believe in totally. Then you must impress on everyone associated with your program that this belief is well founded. Only then will you gain the full commitment of your athletes.

However, this is only the groundwork. If your athletes are to achieve the highest level of performance, you must help them believe they can reach the top. Each swimmer attaining even a personal-best performance

time at the right moment can help make believers out of their teammates.

 THINK TITLES

After winning more than a decade of consecutive state boys' championships at Wilson High School, we had not placed one boy in the finals of the U.S. National Senior Championship meet. We were qualifying boys but not placing them at the meet. We were successful at our state level but not at the national level.

That year my oldest son, Dan, had a hot swim in the 200-yd free and qualified for the big final. I will always remember the surprised look on the faces of the other team members at that meet. For the first time I realized that they did not *expect* to place or to win at the National Championship meet. We had talked about it, but very few believed it could happen. This was the breakthrough we needed. In that meet two additional boys placed in the finals in their individual events. These swimmers believed and expected the best at their state high school meet and at their regional competition. It took one tough team member to get the others to believe in themselves and to succeed at the national level.

Setting Goals

Goals are an extension of your philosophy. They represent the standards that you believe are important and possible. Some goals will be more important to you than others; for example, your philosophy might say that academic achievement takes precedence over athletic achievement. If an athlete's schoolwork is going to be compromised by an athletic event or training, then academic achievement must come first.

In our program we make the connection between philosophy and goals through our mission statement. We tailor this statement each year to meet the specific abilities and personalities of the athletes on the team. The core of the philosophy—what we value most—does not change.

Your success in attaining your goals, not necessarily how much you achieve, will determine how satisfied you are in your coaching position. Percy Cerutty, the great Australian track coach, said, "To be satisfied is to be finished." If you set your sights low and you reach them, you may feel satisfied, but you may not have gained much. However, if you set your sights high and come up a little short, you may not be completely satisfied, but you may have made a significant accomplishment.

In chapter 3 I will explain how to set goals with your team that are ultimately challenging, yet also satisfying. I will distinguish between being satisfied and having a satisfying feeling. Goal-setting is an important process, because it is a means of establishing tangible aspirations that are consistent with your philosophy, principles, and beliefs.

Summary

Coaching and participation in swimming can be very worthwhile if the outlook and expectations of those involved center on what is best for the athletes. In this chapter I presented the means through which coaches can shape their programs to meet the needs of their athletes:

1. Make the athletes on each year's team second only to family.
2. Continue to learn from every means available. Clinics, videos, articles, books, and coaching colleagues are continuous sources.
3. Determine what values are critical to the development of your athletes.
4. Identify the principles you will use to best convey your philosophy.
5. Commit yourself to your principles, and convince your athletes to share your beliefs.

Chapter 2

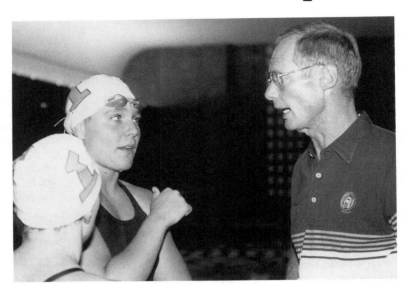

Communicating
Your Approach

You may have the most up-to-date, scientific, and technical information available, and you may know the best there is to know in coaching, but if you do not communicate all that information to your athletes, then it's useless.

This is the *X* factor in coaching. The ability to communicate effectively will determine in large part the success of any coach; it is a skill that can and must be developed throughout your career.

Your style of communication may change as necessary to get your view across. Motivation, discussed in detail in chapter 3, is directly related to communication. The ability to get your ideas across to your swimmers will help to build motivation in all parts of your program.

Successful coaches have a number of identifiable traits, the most important of which is enthusiasm. Great coaches communicate with enthusiasm. They know where they're going, and they know what needs to be done to get there.

Enthusiasm is catching. It affects attitude, work ethics, and a swimmer's personal pride.

 GOOD ADVICE

In the early '70s, Jack Horsley, one of my summer collegiate swimmers who had already been an Olympic bronze medal winner for another club before moving to Tacoma, taught me the importance of enthusiasm. After his second season with me, just before he graduated from college, he said to me, "Coach, don't ever lose

9

your enthusiasm!" Jack said that it was my enthusiasm that had the greatest effect on him as a swimmer. Though a lot of years have gone by, Jack's advice may be some of the best I've ever received.

Communicating With Swimmers

You have beliefs that are vital to your program's success. What is the most effective training for particular events? What is the most efficient technique for each stroke and for each individual? You continually communicate such beliefs to your swimmers, sometimes on the team level and sometimes on the individual level. Whatever methods you choose to convey your beliefs, you must reach the highest percentage possible of the swimmers on your team.

For example, I have to express to my swimmers the importance and necessity of the individualization of training groups. Sometimes each group will have their own special training; some groups may swim less distance or fewer sprints than another. I must make every team member understand that special training is in the best interests of our team in order to best prepare each group for the specific needs of their particular events. Team unity and cooperation are the results of effective communication.

Early season communication could include many of the following:

- The competitive meet schedule
- Attendance policies
- Team standards
- The seasonal training plan
- Warm-up and warm-down procedures
- Goal-setting procedures

Once you've set your schedule, give it to your swimmers and their parents. In one of the first team meetings discuss and explain the schedule. Address such matters as when the team must be ready to swim fast and how they must prepare to reach that goal.

Communication will be necessary throughout the season to keep the team and its members directed toward that championship meet at the end of the season. It is a challenge for the coach to anticipate every swimmer's needs to avoid problems. Everyone must be re-

minded occasionally of the why, where, and how of the program's direction.

 PLATEAUS

Swimmers will not all adapt to your training program at the same rate. Some won't be able to swim fast until they are fully rested, and others will often swim fast during the season. This can become a point of concern by affecting the mental confidence of some of your swimmers, so talk to them when this occurs and keep them focused on the end result.

It always inspires me to hear my swimmers respond with an emphatic yes! when I ask if they believe they can reach their goals at the championship meet even when they are swimming slowly in a dual meet. The great competitors go on to tell me that they know their training times are on schedule and that they will be there when their rest comes in the peak preparation period.

Communication— A Two-Way Street

Your swimmers must believe they can talk to you. They should be able to ask you questions and to get some of the answers. You must provide time for those athletes who need to talk. Almost all swimmers will doubt themselves sometimes, and talking to their coach can dispel those fears and restore their self-confidence, especially when they realize their coach has total confidence in them. Your swimmers will train more effectively when you help them understand the goal of a particular training load, so always be prepared to provide the needed answers to their questions.

As coach, you are the resident expert in helping your swimmers. You must teach your swimmers to come to you first with their questions and concerns. I always tell my swimmers that if I want my car repaired, I don't go to my banker. I also try to convey that I don't have all the answers.

I prefer to meet with my swimmers before or after workout on the pool deck, because there both the swimmer and the coach are in their own environment, and both can resolve any problems the swimmer might have before they are blown out of proportion. I recommend that most team meetings be held before practice, and I prefer to have the individual swimmer meetings after. If you have an office, reserve regular hours for individual meetings.

In the Pool

A large part of swimmer–coach communication actually occurs in the water. Because it can be difficult to hear, get the athletes' attention and make eye contact. Keep it short and simple. Communication may be either a hand signal on their technique, or even an enthusiastic "Right on!" during a hard training set. The important thing is to make your swimmers believe you are watching and evaluating each of them all the time they are swimming.

I used to place myself at different positions around the pool: the ends, the sides, on a high stepladder over the pool, and sometimes in the pool. I think all your swimmers should believe you are watching them during each training session. Many great coaches and swimmers share my view. Coach Dave Robertson told me of his swimming for the legendary Matt Mann at Michigan. When Dave entered the pool, Matt would call out his name, "Robby, how are you today?" Dave got a lift from those training sessions, because Matt cared. Also, former world record holder Coach Mike Troy stated that when he swam for Doc Counsilman at Indiana, he believed Doc was always watching him while he was training. All the other team members also believed Doc watched them.

In the Pool Area, Out of the Water

Team meetings are usually best when there are the fewest distractions. A classroom with comfortable seats and desks is ideal, but the pool deck can be a practical and time-saving location. If the pool has another team, divers, or a class in it, eliminate as much distraction as possible. Pick a corner and have the team face you with a wall behind you.

Make eye contact with each swimmer. Don't talk to them when they are talking to each other. When you get their attention, talk to each swimmer. In your team meetings encourage feedback and ask for questions.

THE SURPRISE QUESTION

In one training session several years ago, I had gone over the training program for that day on the blackboard and had asked my team if they had any questions. One of our team captains asked me why we were doing one particular hard training set; because it was an endurance set, he obviously didn't believe it was necessary for his 100 breaststroke event. My first response was to overreact and excuse him from that practice, but then I decided quickly and emphatically to give him and the team, who were in a state of mild shock, some short, quick, and meaningful reasons why we were doing that set.

Not only was the team captain a leader during the swim set, he did the set enthusiastically. He had a great training session. After practice he came and thanked me for explaining that particular set, and then he went on to say that I was right about doing it. I was happy that I chose to communicate on this occasion instead of overreacting.

Away From the Pool

Many communication opportunities occur on trips and at team social functions. You can sit and talk with team members during the meals and during the drive or flight on road trips. There are also long periods of time to talk at some of the full- or part-day swim competitions, or your swimmers may have an extended period of time between competitions. These are all excellent opportunities to increase the level of communication on your team.

At the Competition

Talking to your swimmers prior to competing will make your communication at competition more meaningful for them. Let your swimmers know what you expect from each of them in warm-up and warm-down. Tell them where to sit and what responsibilities they have while a teammate is competing.

I recommend talking briefly to your swimmers prior to each of their events and soon after they have completed an event. Before the race a brief positive reinforcement of the race strategy and some attention to technique may be in order. The key is not to change the race plan at the last minute. At the conclusion of the race, share with your swimmer the positive aspects of the event, the race splits, and any improvements to be made for the next competition.

Whether it may be necessary to relax your swimmers before their next race, or necessary to excite them, it is your responsibility as coach to let your swimmers know that you are watching their swimming event very closely. Your comments after competition can be critical for your athletes' future success. Be positive but be honest. Be concise yet brief, because there will be time for more details in the next training session.

Though communication should be positive, not every performance is always great. Sometimes we need to be told that we can do better. If a competitive performance is below expectation, it should be put in the proper perspective.

∞ AN HONEST ANSWER

After a competitive race one of my team captains came to me for a postrace evaluation. He asked me, "How was it?" I told him his performance was bad and then I told him why. He had taken the race out too slowly and placed himself in a deep hole. He didn't break out aggressively off the walls on his turns, and he had lost control of the race. I told him that this particular performance was below his level. He didn't like to hear the evaluation, but it was accurate.

A couple of weeks later, after the same event in another dual meet, he had performed very well. He then asked me the same question, and I told him that his performance was great, and why. He then said something that I will never forget: "Coach, remember 2 weeks ago when you told me how bad my race had been? You were right. I didn't like hearing it, but thanks for being honest. It helped!"

COMMUNICATION TIPS WITH THE SWIMMER

- Stress the positive but be honest about the negative.
- Emphasize what they are doing right, and avoid emphasizing what they are doing wrong.
- Use praise to reinforce good performances.
- Correct the swimmer only when he or she can do better.
- Speak to every swimmer during every training session. An ignored swimmer is an unhappy swimmer.
- Coach at the swimmers' eye level or close to it. Kneel, crouch, sit close to the swimmer whenever possible.
- Create pictures with your words. "Arm out front like a spear."
- Be as specific as possible. "Finish the hand of the arm stroke here."
- Use words that are easy to understand.
- Use your body—arms, hands, shoulders, hips, and legs—to emphasize a point.

- Be short and to the point.
- Call your swimmers by name when speaking to them.
- Ask for feedback from the swimmer on technique. How does it feel?
- Concentrate on one point at a time.
- Be patient. If the swimmer hasn't learned, the teacher hasn't taught.

Communicating With Others

Besides your swimmers you need to communicate with others, because your success as a coach will be measured by your peers, colleagues, and various other members of the community. Your ability to converse with these groups can lead to good relationships and can help assure a positive image for your team. What follows is a list of the significant others with whom you will need to communicate to be a more effective coach.

Communicating With Officials

Swimming officials are most often volunteers in the truest sense of the word. They must take the time to study the rules, and then go through a certification process—all in order to assure that no swimmer attains an unfair advantage. I respect the officials, and I want my swimmers to do the same.

If one of my swimmers is disqualified, I want to know the reason for it. Whether I agree or disagree with the official, I must do so in a professional manner. I expect the official to explain the reason for disqualification to me, so that both my swimmer and I can avoid any future disqualification for the same reason. It is up to me as coach to teach my swimmers to compete within the rules.

In any negative officiating situation, ask for the rule interpretation in a nonthreatening manner. Accept the obvious infractions with a "thank you" to the officials. When you catch violations early in the season, you have time to eliminate them before the championship meet. Even if you disagree with the official, give your reasons but accept the ruling graciously.

You should insist that swimmers practice all of their strokes and turns according to the rules. If you permit your swimmers to do illegal turns in practice, then their chances of violating the turn rules in competition are greater. Pay special attention to your swimmers' starts, turns, and finishes; they are critical areas for possible disqualification in competition.

Communicating With Assistants

Communication with your assistant coaches is essential. In high school and college swimming, the assistant and the head coach will most often be on the deck at the same time; however, in club swimming, this is less often the case. Sometimes the assistant will even be at a different pool than the head coach.

Coaches' meetings are a necessity and should be regularly scheduled, with weekly meetings the ideal and monthly the minimum. All coaches must know their responsibilities; they must understand the training program, they must be headed in the same direction, and finally, they must understand the basic technique drills for the week.

I prefer meeting away from the pool, usually a dinner meeting where everyone is more relaxed and there's time for some social interaction. Coaches should have the time to present their views on how to improve the program. Coaches can also report on the progress of their swimmers. I make copies for my assistants of any new coaching materials I acquire, so they have as much information as possible.

You should always make your assistants feel comfortable with providing their input at meetings. You must give your assistants ownership in the team by delegating responsibility to them in the form of coaching assignments. The more responsibility you give them, the greater their stake in the team's success. As a result, they will feel more free to offer suggestions on how to improve the program.

Communicating With Other Coaches

You can learn a great deal from other coaches by keeping the lines of communication open. This is my philosophy: The more willing you are to share your ideas, the more likely other coaches will want to share theirs with you. With such an open-minded view, you will always have a steady source of information available to you.

The high school coach and the club coach of a particular swimmer must communicate, because when both coaches work together to bring the best of both programs to the athlete, they provide the swimmer with the best chance for success. When one of my my Tacoma Swim Club members is on a high school team, I call or visit the coach. This policy is a win–win situation for the swimmer and for the coaches, because the swimmer's chances of improving are better, and the high school coach is more apt to refer new swimmers to the club coach.

Communicating With Parents

Although parents are the most willing and anxious group of people to help their young athletes succeed, they receive too little information about their role as supporters of their athletes. It is your responsibility to guide the parents toward the goal of cooperating with your program.

Whether you are a high school coach, a college coach, or a club coach, parents are part of the team. Usually, however, the younger your team members, the more important their parents become. For example, if the swimmer is too young to drive, then she or he must depend on a parent for transportation. Though the importance of parental involvement varies with the athlete's age, parents remain a vital part of any successful program.

I always try to have a parent-swimmer meeting at the start of each season. I go over the competition schedule, and I invite them to attend every possible swim meet. Then I explain how much time and work is involved in our program; I ask for their help in the "hidden training"—sleep, rest, and nutrition, because for the most part, parents can see better how well the athletes take care of themselves. Then I give the parents a prepared information sheet that contains the most up-to-date, scientific nutrition recommendations for athletes.

Finally, I ask the parents to love their children unconditionally and to be patient with them when evaluating their progress during the season. I then leave them with the assurance that should the need arise, my door is always open to them.

Follow-up socials are usually held sometime during the season and at the awards banquet at the season's end. A monthly newsletter is sent to all club members on our team, detailing most results, special events, a monthly calendar, and coming meets. I try to write a column almost every month, sharing my philosophy and my beliefs with club members.

Communicating With the School Faculty

I coached high school swimming for 30-plus years, and I have coached club swimming almost 40 years and counting. High school swimming differs from club swimming, because it is an extension of the school's academic program. A high school swim team must earn the respect of its faculty and its school administrators, and no one is in a better position to make this happen than the coach. You can support teachers when necessary by setting high eligibility requirements for your swimmers in academic achievement and classroom citizenship. I wanted the faculty members of my high school to support our team, because I knew that every teacher who recognized the accomplishments of one of my swimmers contributed to the potential success of the team.

I sought support from faculty members by requesting that they inform me if any swim team members fell behind in one of their classes. Any swimmer who was in academic trouble in any class was also at risk on the swim team for that period of time, and when it proved necessary, an athlete was denied the privilege to travel or to participate in competition, and even in some cases was barred from our training sessions. I also informed faculty members that I expected my swimmers to be good citizens in their classes.

Setting such high standards earned for our team the respect of our school faculty and administrators. Many of the best teachers in our high school attended our major competitive meets, and when they returned to class, often praised our swimmers' performances.

In fact, some of the greatest support we ever received was from our faculty. Our bleachers, acoustical tile, and other equipment were built by faculty members of our high school; our faculty presented water shows to students and parents over at least 3 years. The faculty did skits in and out of the water to raise money for special pool projects. It was great fun for all of us. The celebration party we had after the show each year also contributed to our school morale, creating a closer faculty and administration, as well as benefiting our swim team.

Communicating With the Student Body

The student body needs to be proud of the high school swim team. A winning tradition helps, but it will not stand forever by itself. There are many ways to cultivate student body support. For example, in our first years I gave bonus points to those students in my physical education classes who attended swim meets. Getting people to the competition was the first step to attracting even more people. We built one meet, the Ram Relays, held every year just after Christmas, into a yearly tradition by having sales contests for our swim team members, with prizes for those selling the most Ram Relays' tickets. The school pep band played to turn-away crowds almost every year that we had our contests.

My first year the school yearbook had one page for the swim team. By lobbying the student editors and the faculty advisor, we brought the yearbook section on the swim team to eight pages within a few years.

Then, there was that student reporter who was responsible for covering swimming in the school newspaper. *That* reporter got the red carpet treatment from this swim coach. The Wilson High School swim team was all over the sports page of the school newspaper in every possible issue.

Former Wilson students who are nonswim team members still come up to me in the community and compliment our great Wilson swim teams. Such student body pride helped keep swimming important in our high school.

Communicating With the Media

The media is your swim team's link to the community. Will Rodgers once said that all that he knew he read in the newspapers. Today you can add radio and television to that. You can have the best program in swimming, but unless you get media support, very few members of your community will know about it.

During my first years of coaching, I had to build media support by hand delivering the results of our swim meets to the sports department of our local newspaper. Though my deliveries were usually in the evening and never convenient for me, I became acquainted with each of the sports reporters and the sports editor. My relationship with the editors really helped as we built a winning tradition. When our first swimmer competed in the Olympics, the local newspaper sent a sportswriter to cover the event.

In 1968 our Tacoma Swim Club placed a swimmer, Kaye Hall, on the U.S. Olympic Team. She was also a Wilson High School student. She won the 100-m backstroke event in Mexico City. Her world record, two gold medals, and one bronze medal assured Tacoma swimming programs of strong media attention for many years to come.

    A NIGHT CALL

I still remember being awakened in the middle of the night in Mexico City by a telephone call from a Tacoma city official after Kaye Hall's Olympic victory. He was in charge of a planned media event, the homecoming celebration of Kaye's return to Tacoma. Suddenly, our swimming success was receiving media attention and I couldn't help but reflect on those years of my personally handing our swim meet results to the local newspaper.

ACQUIRING THE COOPERATION OF YOUR LOCAL MEDIA

- Consider the media to be a top priority after the meet. Call or hand deliver your meet results to local radio, television, and newspapers as soon as possible after the meet. Be prepared to deliver some good quotes and possibly have a very successful swimmer available for comments.
- Know your media deadlines and be sure to meet them. If you are on the road, phone in meet results before returning home, because a day late won't make it.
- Call whether you win or lose; it will help establish and build your credibility.
- Understand a newspaper's space and time restraints and be aware of slow news days. If basketball or football fill the sports pages on Saturdays and Sundays, but the paper runs features on Thursdays, you have a better chance of getting your story in on the slower day.
- Find a kid on your team with a great human interest story, like overcoming some sort of handicap, achieving a high academic record, or excelling in another area.
- Look for media outlets that feature "athletes of the week" and find out how to get your athletes considered for the honor.
- About four or five days before a swim meet, call a sportswriter who covers swimming with details of the coming meet. You may just hit the right moment for additional coverage.

Benefits of a Supportive Community

The pride of our Wilson High School alumni grew to be a positive factor in our community. In addition to school pride, the success of our Wilson High School swim teams, and the national and international attention of our Tacoma Swim Club swimmers did much to communicate positive values to our community. For example, our Wilson High School swim team received two Washington State Senate Commendations at the state capitol, and both our high school and club swimmers received numerous commendations at the county, city, and school district levels.

While our community honored us, we reached out to others. Tacoma Swim Club hosted swim teams from Germany, Norway, England, Hong Kong, and Japan over a period of time. Newspaper articles of these exchanges brought it to the attention of our community.

The benefits of communicating, either through action or words, with your community are many. For example, when we went to organizations and individuals in our community with projects to benefit swimming in Tacoma, we were successful. Our community aided in the purchase of an automatic timing system for our 10-lane pool in the Metropolitan Park District of Tacoma, and also helped in raising the money for the Tacoma Swim Club to travel to international competitions and exchanges.

Summary

The principles of communicating effectively as a swim coach can be summed up as follows:

1. Effective communication is vital to a swim team's success. This is the X factor in coaching.
2. Your style of motivation may change to fit the needs of the occasion or of the swimmer.
3. Enthusiasm is essential to communicating effectively.
4. Communication is a two-way street. Swimmers must feel they can come to the coach, so keep the door open to all.
5. Effective communication anticipates problems and eliminates any potential problems.
6. Communication in the pool is best when short and to the point.
7. Swimmers have to believe the coach is always watching and evaluating them.
8. Make eye contact whenever possible.
9. Recognize the opportunities to communicate: team trips, dinners, and the like.
10. Talk to your swimmers both as a team and as individuals, according to need.
11. Be positive but be *honest!*
12. Talk to the swimmers before, during, and after the competition to help them maintain focus.
13. Communicate with everyone who can help: parents, faculty, media, school.
14. Effective communication can be built on the positive accomplishments of your team.

Chapter 3

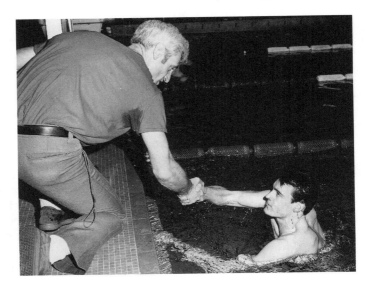

Motivating Swimmers

Swimming is an individual sport with team ramifications. At the high school and college levels, it becomes much more team-oriented, because the points that each swimmer scores contribute to team victories. It is easier to motivate swimmers when the successful completion of their goals contributes to those of the team.

However, motivating swimmers as part of a team often presents challenges not found in other sports. The nature of the sport itself requires that swimmers usually go through a period of preparation that is more individually oriented. The swimmer is isolated from the coach by water, unable to see or hear very much or talk to anyone while swimming. There is less extrinsic motivation in swimming than in other sports. For example, there are no balls to bounce, throw, or catch as, say, in basketball. Rewards in

the pool come less frequently than they do on a basketball court; there's no swish of a ball passing through the hoop; most often, there's only more water, more turns, and more strokes. That's why swimmers, perhaps more than any other athletes, need meaning, motivation, and fun in order to persist, and it's our responsibility as coaches to help them find these necessary elements.

What Motivation Is

I can sum up my idea of motivation within our program very simply: If we can sustain intensive training and have fun doing it, then we have the necessary motivation. When swimmers and coach excitedly come to each practice session and train with enthusiasm,

17

then they have the motivation. If this is the case in your program, don't worry about fixing it; it isn't broken.

Coach Motivation Versus Swimmer Motivation

Coach and swimmer motivation is like the chicken and the egg riddle: Which came first? I've always told my swimmers that they create the excitement, and that if they want their coach to be enthusiastic and excited at training and competition, then do something thrilling. Swim fast!

I motivate my swimmers by urging them to generate some excitement. I get them thinking about their own responsibility to motivate themselves, but this doesn't let me off the hook; it just gives me another tool to encourage my swimmers.

How can you get motivated unless the swimmers are? I always say that motion creates emotion. As coach you shouldn't be like a plow horse pulling a buckboard of swimmers up a steep hill; rather, you should be like someone trying to hold onto the back end of a train's caboose that's under a full head of steam and going full speed downhill. Your swimmers stoke the engine with the fuel of their effort, and you do your best to keep the process going.

In other words, don't pull the motivation load by yourself. Inspire your swimmers and you will be taken along for a most exciting journey, and when they lack the necessary motivation, give them a purpose for their efforts.

Developing Purpose

The greatest thrill swimmers can experience is to swim fast at the championship meet. No matter how much fun they have in the social and competitive events of a swim season, their fun's diminished by swimming slow at the championship meet, so prepare swimmers to do their best in the season finale. This is your purpose in training and you can use it throughout the season to keep practice exciting. There's nothing like looking back on a season of training culminated by a successful championship meet.

    A PURPOSEFUL ANSWER

I give my swimmers questionnaires so they can provide feedback for the program. On one questionnaire I asked, "What is boring in our training program?" Most of the team looked for and found something that was boring for them in their program—long warm ups, long kicking sets, etc.—but one very perceptive swimmer answered, "Nothing is boring in our training. Everything that we do has a purpose."

I received that questionnaire more than 20 years ago, and I have never forgotten it. Everything we do in training should be important, and it will be exciting when it has a purpose.

Though you may have the best plan in the world, if your swimmers do not see the purpose of it, they won't be motivated, and you won't succeed. Making your swimmers aware of the reasons for your training regimen remains a necessity in any program.

It's easy to get excited about fast swimming, but it's important to remember that swimming speed is relative to each swimmer—a slow swim for one might be a fast swim for another. Recognize each swimmer's personal-best practice and competition swims. Praise the successes and teach your swimmers to do likewise to their teammates. Remind your swimmers occasionally throughout the season why they are on the team—to swim fast—and where they are headed.

Developing a Sixth Sense

Knowing when a swimmer or your team needs special motivation is a sixth sense in coaching. Develop the ability to recognize when a swimmer or the team needs reviving. Change your training sessions when you sense they are becoming too routine. For example, if you're afraid your freestyle swimmer might become stale, change him or her to individual-medley training sets for a period of time, or you might hold a team meeting to inspire your swimmers.

There are a number of signals you can see from your swimmers that indicate the need for motivation. If they act lethargic on arrival, sit with their heads drooped, get into the water too slowly, disregard the assigned-time-interval, or act generally disinterested, then they are ready for a motivational transfusion.

Sources of Motivation

Swimmers haven't changed much in my 40-plus years of coaching. Every young athlete wants something—usually some special and personal success. An athlete's desire may be buried deep inside, and he or she may be afraid to admit it, but make no mistake; it is there someplace.

Look at the success of the Superman, Rocky, Rambo, and Karate Kid movies; they are all about winning. Everyone fantasizes about being successful, but the problem is that few athletes seriously consider and devote the effort required to achieve their dreams. Will they do what they have to do, day in and day out, to succeed? Will they stay motivated to train and to push themselves during those water workouts in which they have only their own thoughts to keep them going? These are the questions you have to pose to your swimmers.

Personal Drive

Personal drive is the greatest source of motivation. All athletes have a background of habits already formed before they become a member of your team. Long before you have the opportunity to coach them, your prospective athletes are learning from their parents how to work hard and to be persistent. In many respects, great parents make great coaches, but it is you, the coach, who has the opportunity to ignite that spark of personal drive in each athlete. By establishing goals for your swimmers, you can set their personal drive on fire.

 TIME STANDARDS

Unlike my earlier years of coaching, time standards now exist for qualification to enter particular meets at almost all levels of swimming competition. This built-in goal-setting procedure has a great impact on swimmers. Every age-group swimmer knows the time necessary to move up one classification, and every coach knows the effect that these standards have on their swimmers' personal drive.

Swimmers' Development and Success

An athlete who achieves is a motivated athlete, so teach the basics and gradually move to higher competitive levels according to your athlete's development. Many small successes will motivate your swimmers and give them confidence, allowing them to persevere through those setbacks that do occur.

Swimmers can also motivate themselves with their own individual successes. A swimmer who attains a goal usually wants to attempt to reach a new one at a higher level. Therefore, you have to acknowledge success in your swimmers, regardless of the level at which they are succeeding. Encouragement for a good practice or competition might be a pat on the back, a handshake, or just a "thumbs up," but you should do it soon after each success. In this way, you build your swimmers' confidence not only by recognizing their successes but also by reinforcing those correct techniques that yielded improvement. Thus, as your swimmers attain greater skills through correct practice, they become more confident in competition.

 SUCCESS BUILDS SUCCESS

Our unbeaten record at Wilson High School stretched through 24 years. When our team first started that streak, I feared that the media was putting too much pressure on them, but as it turned out, I was wrong; the problem was mine. I had to adjust to become comfortable with the attention that went with winning almost all of the time. The best part was that it helped us avoid complacency. Our teams, and even our opponents, expected us to win.

External Influences

Through observations, questionnaires, and individual conferences with my athletes, I have drawn some conclusions about external influences. The greatest outside source of motivation during training is the athlete's teammates. Athletes are pushed to their training limits according to the effort and the encouragement of their teammates.

The coach also plays a strong role in testing the athlete's limits. The wise coach will promote an environment that utilizes the motivational potential of teammates. For example, you can arrange the lane assignments to best challenge the swimmers in each lane or place swimmers in head-to-head training on occasion. By increasing the level of competition among teammates, you encourage them to perform at their best.

"Hidden training," the sleep, rest, and nutrition of your young athletes, also plays an important role in motivation. Parents usually tell me that the coach has the most influence in this regard, but swimmers tell me the parents provide the most direction, and the coach is a close second. Regardless of who has the most influence, you need to help parents be aware of what they can do. A home with plentiful supplies of the proper foods and a reasonable curfew can make the difference between the success and failure of your swimmer.

Motivational Tools

Positive motivational quotations are excellent. One favorite of mine is, "Turkeys flock together, and eagles fly alone," and another, "If you are prepared, you won't be scared." Such messages serve as constant reminders of the direction every team member should be headed. I used to pin poster-size motivational messages on the team bulletin board, changing the quotation every few days.

👓 FORTUNE COOKIE MOTIVATION

One night at a Chinese restaurant I received, in my fortune cookie, the motivational message, "You are going on an important journey." It was just before the start of the high school season. I posted the fortune cookie message on the bulletin board. To my surprise, our team not only noticed it, but read it with great interest. Because it was smaller than the typical message, it had grabbed their attention.

This marked the beginning of many years of the Fortune Cookie Corner on our bulletin boards. I would rotate inspirational quotations reduced to the size of a fortune cookie message every few days. The idea grew. Team members submitted fortune-cookie-size quotations for the bulletin board. We had contests for the most motivational quotations each week and for the season. The team members voted on the winners themselves. The process itself became a motivational event, and it bonded our team together.

When we were going for our 24th consecutive state championship meet, fortune-cookie-size messages were all over the place, with the number 24 in nearly all of them. When I picked up the telephone, 24 would be under the receiver. When I opened the door, I might find 24 on the doorknob. I'd started it but it was our team members who'd carried it through the season. There was no chance of them losing sight of the "fortune" we sought.

Books, tapes, articles, and illustrations can all have a role in motivation. I have played motivational audio and video tapes with great success, and I copy and hand out articles to my team frequently.

However, because tapes take time away from training, you should use them infrequently or recommend that swimmers play them at home. Books, particular chapters in books, and articles are also best given to swimmers to read on their own. Avoid using training time for anything other than training.

Speakers

Speakers are a very good motivational source. Our team members can relate to those athletes who have gone through our program and have been successful. Some of these previous athletes were not fast, successful swimmers, but they did very well in their careers. All credited their career successes to their swimming experiences as a member of our team. Over the long run such testimonials from previous swimmers in our program had the greatest impact. Successful swimmers or other athletes outside of your program are the next best choice as motivational speakers.

👓 ADVERSITY AND SUCCESS

This past year one of our former swimmers, Saadi Ghatan, spoke to our club banquet on motivation. Saadi had been a successful swimmer for both Wilson High School and Tacoma Swim Club. He talked about how his time in our program helped prepare him for handling adversity and achieving success outside of swimming.

At one point in his swimming career, Saadi had tried to make the Junior National Championship time standard in the 200-yd backstroke. On the final day of competition in the last available qualifying swim meet, he failed to make the standard in the prelims and in the finals, and even when he took two more time trials after the meet was over. All of his swims were within a few tenths of a second of qualifying. At the time one of his teammates told me that she felt sorry for Saadi. I told her to forget about the pity, that Saadi would be tougher and more determined because of the experience—and he was. He went on to swim in both the Junior and Senior National Championship meets, as well as the NCAA Division I Championship meet.

About six years later, Saadi was rejected by all the medical schools to which he had applied for admission. He was faced with the decision to change his professional goals or to try again. He returned to school for additional science courses, and two years later he was accepted to medical school. He was in his final year at the University of Washington Medical School at the time that he spoke to our swimmers and now is a doctor.

Inspirational Events and Experiences

Every coach would like to believe that the present team will respond to such inspirational stories as Saadi's. I use them in many of my own team meetings, but whenever possible, I use recent experiences that involve the present team members, because their interest level is higher when the story relates to or involves one of them.

The Power of Goals

Successful coaches and swimmers have both a pressing need to excel, and a clear vision of where they are going and what they are doing. Goals are the motivational foundation of a winning season. You and your swimmers must have real, vivid, living goals that will keep you going through every temporary setback that might occur.

OUR FIRST NATIONAL CHAMPIONSHIP MEET

At our first AAU Senior National Championship, our team of four swimmers failed to qualify for any final events; all of them ended near or at the bottom. It was a humiliating experience for me, having been a consistent winner in our state and regional competitions, but it made me more determined than ever to reach our goals of scoring and winning at the national championship. I had to restate and reaffirm my goals that my swimmers would go beyond just qualifying to enter the championship meet. I was determined to qualify swimmers, but I needed to go the additional step and place them at the meet. It would take better organization, planning, effort, and determination. We did just that and had a national champion in the next meet.

Goals keep everyone on target. In my case, goals provide direction; they commit me to the work, time, pain, and whatever else is part of the price of achieving success. Goals provided me the energy and drive to accomplish the task of producing great swimmers.

The key to goal-setting is this: Your objectives must be high enough to excite you, yet not so high that you cannot vividly imagine achieving them. You should be comfortable with and confident in your goals and able to see yourself attaining them, even though they are just out of reach for now.

Setting Team Goals

As coach you must realistically assess the team's opportunities for the coming season. In high school and college, you may strive for the highest possible team finish at the league, state, or national championship. In club swimming, team placement in a championship meet might be a possible goal, or you might hope to qualify a specific number of swimmers for the Regional, Zone, Junior National, or Senior National championships.

Whatever your goals may be, you and your team have to agree that they are reachable and worthy of your best efforts. Your swimmers should believe that they have joined the process of determining the team goals. Great teams are made up of ordinary people who have given an extraordinary effort to accomplish their goals.

THE BIG GOAL—#24

In my final year of coaching high school swimming, I had a typical preseason meeting with the members of the team. We listed our dual meet competition and our championship meet competition and discussed the benefits of a full and complete season of training. We agreed that winning the state championship had to be our primary goal.

Our plan was to use every meet as preparation to win our 24th consecutive state championship title. The team also felt pressure to maintain an unbeaten record through our dual meets as we had done over those 24 years, but that was secondary to another title.

We agreed we would train through all dual and district meets prior to the state meet. This meant training the day of and usually after each competition leading up to state. Our team knew that one of the dual meets would be very difficult to win, but we decided that if we rested for that meet, it would impact our state meet. And so we competed, losing a close dual meet and ending our unbeaten record to an out-of-state team, David Douglas High School of Gresham, Oregon.

However, we were not distracted by this loss. We went on to swim one of our best ever state championship meets. Every swimmer who went to the state meet from that team placed in the top six in their individual events, breaking several state and school records in the process. We won our 24th consecutive title, thanks in part to our preseason decision to focus on our primary goal regardless of setbacks.

Goal-Setting Principles

Setting performance standards is the first step toward achievement, so you want your athletes to use goal-setting methods that have worked time and again. These are the principles I emphasize to my swimmers:

- State your goal positively.
- Be specific and lock yourself in to the end result.
- Avoid setting time limits on some goals. This will keep open the possibility that your swimmers can have long range goals that do not have a time limit and short ones that do have a time limit.
- Keep personal goals to yourself or limit the people with whom you share them to only those who can help you attain your goals. You should always know the objectives of your athletes, so you can relate their training to their goals' attainment. Race-pace swims are one example, because these must relate to the goal time.
- Reset your goals as you approach or attain the present one.

My first organized thoughts on goal-setting came through a business friend of mine more than two decades ago. He loaned me an Earl Nightingale record called "The Strangest Secret." Basically, Nightingale states that people with goals succeed because they know where they are going. The key to success is believing. Believe and you will succeed.

Earl Nightingale outlined these steps for setting goals. Picture a goal in your mind, and think of it in a relaxed way. Write it down on a card and carry it with you for 30 days. Look at it several times a day. Stop thinking all negative thoughts about the goal, replacing them with positive ones. Take control for 30 days, confident that you can achieve the goal, and it will become a reality. I still use these concepts as the basics for my goal-setting.

Setting Swimmer Goals

Some coaches set goals for their swimmers; I usually don't. I can get the wheels turning in their heads, but I can't determine what

they will strive for. The goal has to come from the swimmer to receive commitment from him or her. In other words, I can suggest but they must invest.

For example, I gave my swimmers a chart that listed the following information: the American and the National High School record for all swimming events, the current qualifying times necessary to swim at the Senior and the Junior National Championships, and finally, the state high school championship, and the league or district championship meets. I also would include the necessary time standards for All-American selection, and the current state and varsity records. I would list the top six swimming times in each event, as well as the consolation finals of the previous year's state championship. I gave them the chart each year and then let them use it to build their own dreams.

Dreams Transformed Into Goals

Early in the preseason I talked about dreams and about goals. I would have my swimmers list about 10 or more things that they wanted to accomplish this coming season. I then had them list those things in measurable and specific terms; for example, "I want to win the state championship in the 100-yd freestyle," or "I want to swim 46.80 in the 100-yd freestyle."

My next step was to have them prioritize the top two or three goals from their list. These were to be the most important goals for the swimmers, and they would write them in their logbooks, on their study lamps, on the bathroom mirror, or inside their locker doors. They would carry these goals, see them, and dream about them frequently for a few weeks, and when they truly believed that they could attain their stated goals, they would sit down with me, and I would write their goals into my personal training logbook.

Reasons Lead to Commitment

The primary step of goal-setting is to have the swimmers list their reasons for wanting to reach their objectives. It took me many years to add this step to our goal-setting process, but when I finally did, it resulted in greater commitment by the athletes, as these examples indicate: "I want my parents to be very proud of me," and "I want to feel good about the results of my own hard work," and finally, "I want to attain a college scholarship time."

The reasons for a goal are often more important than the goal itself, because reasons lead to commitment. Swimmers who can visualize how it feels to win, to make the finals, or to do their best time are often highly motivated. However, seeing the time and the place on the scoreboard, the cheering crowd, and the congratulations of their teammates can also lead swimmers to greater commitment.

 GOLD, NOT BRONZE

Brian Goodel, Olympic gold medalist and world record holder, told me that during his training sessions leading up to the 1976 Olympic Games, he pretended to be in the Olympics. He would always see himself, on the top step of the award stand, receiving the gold medal around his neck. The United States flag would be raised, while the Star Spangled Banner played. These images motivated him during the long and hard training sessions preparing him for the 1500-m freestyle in the coming Olympic Games.

At the Olympic Games in Montreal, Brian was trailing two swimmers with 400 m remaining in the race. He said he was tired and thought about how third place and a bronze medal was not so bad. But then his thoughts came immediately back to that image of his being the gold medal winner. That same picture in his mind of winning, that helped him during his training, gave him the motivation and the determination to come from behind, win the event, and break the world record in the process.

Monitor the Process

I recommend meeting with your swimmers at the start of the season to initiate the goal-setting process and to record their goals. Reexamine their goals at midseason and again just before the championship meet. It may be necessary to adjust a goal because of an injury or illness. In most cases swimmers will remain committed to their objectives. Monitor the training necessary to help your swimmers reach their aims. When you've locked their workout regimens into place, be a contributor, a teacher, and a cheerleader for the athletes.

Setting Coach Goals

Although most of us are in coaching for the right reasons, we need goals too in order to provide direction and focus to our programs.

Most coaches take some kind of break—a few weeks or months, depending on whether they are in a school or club program—where they usually discover that there are other things in life outside of coaching swimming. I tend to get a little lazy during these periods, but with specific goals, I can get back a strong work ethic for the next season. I visualize the team and myself achieving our goals, and I get excited about starting a new year.

 AN EXAMPLE FROM EXPERIENCE

The greatest test in setting goals for myself at the beginning of a new high school season came just after my first Olympic Games experience. I was on the airplane returning from the Mexico City Olympics. It had been a long season of preparation for the Olympic Trials and all of the other competition leading into the Olympic Games. One of our team members, Kaye Hall, had just won two gold medals, one bronze, and had set a new world record for the 100-m backstroke.

Naturally, my spirits were higher than the 35,000 ft at which we were flying, but my body and mind were exhausted. I had just been through 2 years of preparation for the Olympic Trials and the Olympic Games, and now I had to begin a new season of boys' high school swimming almost as soon as the plane landed. I began to write down a possible competitive meet lineup for the coming season, and I started to dream about what those particularly talented young boys could do before the end of their high school careers. I listed our team goals and what I thought each swimmer could do that year. I formed teaching plans and training objectives for that season. I believed we could win the state championship with this young team just in their first year of high school swimming, and I could picture it vividly as I flew home.

That airplane ride seemed very short. I became very excited about getting started again in a new season, and when that airplane landed in Seattle, I hit the ground running. Suddenly I was enthusiastic again, and I can remember the feeling even now after 25 years. That year we won our 10th consecutive boys' state championship, and two years later in those boys' senior year, we won every event except the 50-yd free at the state high school championship meet.

Results of Goals

Goal-setting should be an exciting process, because it dares you to reach new personal horizons. Excitement also comes from the intensive training necessary to attain objectives, and from their actual achievement. Establishing and seeking goals can give meaning to your coaching, to your team's effort, and to the swimmers' efforts in training and competition. Exploring your reasons for attaining goals helps provide your commitment and helps sustain your motivation. Furthermore, the benefits of this process carry over to all phases of the swimmers' lives. Setting goals works in school, on the job, in relationships, and throughout life. My 89-year-old mother has goals; she is always scheduling a dinner for friends, planning a trip, or doing something meaningful. She lives each day to the fullest and is excited about the future.

I believe that the way we had set goals was one of the reasons our high school swimmers did so well in school. Our swim team had the highest grade point average of all the athletic teams in our school almost every year. More than 95% of our swimmers went to college, and a very high percentage of those graduated. Great swimmers manage their time well and succeed both academically and in the pool.

 MY FAMILY EXPERIENCE

My wife and I have four children, Dan, Dave, Dick, and Debby, who benefited tremendously from the athletic and academic goals they set. All of them swam at the Senior National Championship level. The three boys were state champions, All-American swimmers in high school and college, and world-ranked in their events. Yet because their goals extended beyond the pool, all four were motivated to achieve in their schoolwork and careers. Dan and Debby are lawyers, Dave is a dentist, and Dick a high school teacher and principal. As my family illustrates, setting goals has value for a lifetime.

Attaining and Sustaining Goals

After the athletes' goals are properly set, the focus of the total program shifts to reaching them. It is your job to effectively organize the athletes' training time. Your swimmers must feel that all activities scheduled for them will help them succeed.

Throughout training the primary source of swimmers' motivation must come from within them, and not from you. The swimmer has the power to choose how fast he or she will swim a particular training set, as well as the ability to select the best send-off time he or she can attain on an appropriate training set.

As coach you can give rewards to swimmers who attain goal times or take major steps toward those times in practice. Rewards help reinforce the swimmers' determination to succeed, and they keep the swimmers more highly motivated during training sets.

Persistence in the pursuit of goals is an important characteristic of successful swimmers, coaches, and teams. When the stress of a long swim season begins to lower your team's motivational intensity, you must recognize it and adjust your program accordingly.

Rewards

Rewards don't have to be of material or monetary value; the greatest rewards are usually the easiest to give. Meaningful attention from the coach is a great reward. When you look into the eyes of a young athlete, and express your recognition of their exceptional effort, you give them a significant reward. It can also be one of your finest moments in coaching.

The greatest reward I get from my swimmers is a simple thank you. The swimmer who comes up after an intensive training session and says, "Thanks coach for a great workout," does more to motivate me than anything else in my coaching.

The first material reward I gave for a good training set was a small piece of smoked salmon. In the Pacific Northwest, this was probably the best treat available.

Recognition also means a lot to athletes. Recognize their efforts and try to keep it simple. I have also used a season-long point table as a reward. I will detail this in chapter 6 under tips for making practices fun.

Discipline

There are fewer opportunities available for young people today to acquire good discipline. Athletics remains one of the best sources for learning discipline.

Discipline has many definitions, one of which involves exercising strict control to enforce obedience. Another type of discipline comes from encouraging the gradual development of self-control, orderly conduct, character, and new habits. My swim programs have always functioned best under this second form of discipline. Swim training requires self-control over an extended period of time, before the thrills of competition take place. In addition to training, your athletes must develop self-control in their personal and social habits. In other words, establish for your swimmers those standards of conduct that will contribute most to the success of your team. For example, you might make attendance in school a requirement for participation in competition. Your standards should include making passing grades the minimum requirement for participation. You should also establish policies against smoking cigarettes, drinking alcohol, or using other recreational drugs.

However, team standards should also focus on the positive. Your swimmers' pride is best built on a solid foundation. Ask yourself, Can this team be its best without standards? Great swimmers demonstrate their discipline by choosing to attend practice, train diligently, study hard in the classroom, and adhere to the team standards.

Disciplinary Action

As coach it's your responsibility to step in when the athletes fail to govern themselves. You must be prepared to make some hard decisions. Whatever disciplinary actions you may take, make sure they're fair and consistent. Be willing to discipline your fastest swimmer to the same degree as you would your slowest.

Your best corrective discipline for an athlete should never be considered punishment; rather, it must be a learning experience. I never disciplined athletes in such a way that they could not return to the team at some point. I made it clear that it was their mistakes that necessitated disciplinary measures. I also would tell them that we could put it all behind us and that they had the opportunity to be reinstated as a full team member again at some point in the future.

I have suspended athletes for the remainder of a given season when necessary for a major infraction, but I always allowed them the opportunity to return to the club or school team the next season. Whenever a suspension was necessary, it was because the infraction violated our team's written code of ethics.

Personally I don't like too many rules; I prefer standards, because, unlike rules, which are often things to be broken, standards are something to be attained. Some standards are necessary if the swimmers are to develop a strong sense of team pride.

In my 32 years of high school coaching, our team standards always included refraining from the use of alcohol and other recreational drugs during the swim season. I didn't go out of my way to be an enforcer of the standards, because I didn't have to. In any high school violations have a way of being brought to the attention of the coach.

Sure, I suspended athletes for failing to live by our standards, but it was not often necessary. On the club level I have sent a swimmer home by airplane prior to the completion of the competition, because that swimmer failed to abide by the team standards of behavior on trips. The fact that I was willing to suspend when necessary helped to minimize this type of behavior. Actually I had to resort to such drastic measures only about six or seven times over 40-plus years of coaching. The discipline I find most beneficial for athletes is acquired in small steps day by day. Developing the habits of perseverance, hard work, competitiveness, and resilience require this gradual form of discipline.

My form of discipline has more to do with accomplishing the things that need to be done than it does with avoiding the things that violate team standards. Discipline comes through maintaining self-control and choosing to make the most of your competitive swimming experience. Don't leave home without it—discipline!

Summary

Motivation is vital to keep swimmers consistently on the road to success. The following are very effective components of motivation:

1. Fast swimming always motivates.
2. The innate desire to succeed is the best foundation to build upon.

3. Personal drive is the greatest source of motivation.
4. Success can breed more successes.
5. Teammates are the major motivators in training.
6. The swimmer is the major motivator in competition.
7. Motivational quotations are valuable tools.
8. Speakers can play a major motivational role.
9. Goals motivate.
10. Goals provide the direction and the destination.
11. The reasons for wanting a goal lead to commitment.
12. The goal-setting process must be continually monitored.
13. The coach must set goals.
14. Goals provide excitement in the swim program.
15. The greatest rewards are the easiest to give, such as meaningful attention.
16. Discipline is a major success factor in swimming.
17. Discipline should be built around team standards, not rules.

Chapter 4

Building a Swimming Program

In swimming we have several types of programs, including high school, college, and club. Club swimming involves U.S. teams and YMCA teams, which have many similarities. High school and college teams have a shorter swim season than club teams, and they allow student athletes to compete only for their high school or collegiate years. Masters swimming, which is also gaining in popularity, provides a lifetime of competitive opportunities.

Club swimming is long-term and can be a cradle-to-the-grave program if it provides for masters swimmers. High school and collegiate athletes will usually continue to swim for their club teams during their high school and college years. In high school this usu-

ally means the swimmer competes for the club team, except for the three months of the high school season. In some states the high school swimmer can compete for the club during the season, as long as it does not conflict with the high school schedule. College swimmers may swim for their club while their college is not in session, usually in the summer.

Most of my high school coaching career included only three years of high school swimming for each athlete. In my final years at Wilson High School, I had the swimmers for four years.

Tacoma Swim Club was another story; I actually had some swimmers on the team for 20 years, like my sons Dan and Dave

27

who competed from ages 5 to 25. Both Dan and Dave swam for Tacoma Swim Club long enough to complete their studies at law and dental school, respectively. Dave swam at the University of Southern California and Dan at the University of Washington, but during the summers of their undergraduate and graduate years, they swam on Tacoma Swim Club.

Because of the differences in their length of seasons—a high school's is only about 3 months, whereas a club's can last as long as 11 months or more—high school and club programs should be built differently. Of course, the length of the season isn't the only thing that differentiates coaching a high school team from a club team. In this chapter I'll explain what it takes to build and maintain both types of programs.

Building a High School Program

A high school swim team will be better when you have a good base of swimmers who have competed in club age-group swimming, but you must also take advantage of the many good athletes already in school who have not had previous competitive swimming experience. All of my successful teams at Wilson High School used just such a mix of swimmers.

Recruiting Swimmers

Swimming is usually not a school sport for pre–high school students. The best athletes in the school may have been playing other sports in elementary, middle, or junior high school, so you must do more than just announce that the swimming team will begin practice on a specific date.

When I was a business education teacher, I traded teaching stations with the physical education teacher for one or two days in order to test the times of the advanced swimmers for 50 yd in the crawl, the breaststroke, the butterfly, and the backstroke. Such advanced swimmers were always our best source of potential competitors.

When I became a physical education teacher, I placed the students into groups according to their tested swimming ability. The advanced swimmers remained together as a unit through each specialty of the physi-

cal education classes, and most importantly, they swam together at the same time at the start of the school year for a specified number of weeks. This gave me the opportunity to teach advanced swimming skills to them for three to six weeks each semester. I then tested the advanced swimmers at the end of their swimming section for 50 yd in each of the four competitive strokes, thus providing me with a list of prospective swim team members. Finally, I met with each of the prospects and gave them a written invitation to join our swim team. We gained many new swimmers each year this way, many of whom became state champions and All-Americans at Wilson High School.

    ONE P.E. CLASS SUCCESS

I still remember my first success story in recruiting from a physical education class. Rick Erspamer, a first-year swimmer, placed at the state championship. His physical education class tests were not outstanding; in fact, he wasn't at the top of the timed tests. Even his best test in the 50-yd breaststroke wasn't very fast, but his great breaststroke kick caught my eye, so I recruited him.

Rick decided to give swimming a try, even though he hadn't previously considered it, and he went on to win and set state records in his final two years at Wilson High School in the 100-yd breaststroke. This happened early in my career at Wilson High School and set a pattern for all of my high school coaching years. I continued these tests each year, with many additional success stories, until I retired from high school coaching.

The most important source of swimmers is the swim clubs and YMCA teams that may be in your community. The swimmers who have had age-group competitive experience are usually the foundation of a successful high school team, because they already have some of the necessary skills and are usually the most receptive to an invitation to join your swim team. The Tacoma Swim Club, which I started in 1955, was the feeder system for my Wilson High School teams.

Team Levels

A high school swim team may have only varsity competition. If enough swimmers are on the team, and reserve competition is available, then reserve swim team experience should be offered. Wilson High School did have a reserve

swim team for many years, but competition from other schools became very scarce.

Each swimmer's time for a particular event determines who swims the event in competition. Your fastest swimmers in each event could most often swim that event, especially in a closely contested swim meet. Instituting a program for each ability level is more important for training than it is for competition. The strongest and fastest swimmers can gain the most from having adequate pool time available. Also the pool and deck space of each individual pool will determine the number of swimmers at each level. Your highest ability group must have the most pool time.

When necessary, I would group our team into three training levels depending on the ability and the number of swimmers. I actually had 65 boys on the Wilson High School team one year, and I was the only coach at that time. I ran this three-level training program to maximize the available space. I will detail this practice in chapter 6.

Gaining Faculty and Administration Support

The support of your faculty and administration is often the result and not the cause of success in a swim program. If your swimmers are excellent students and citizens in school, they will receive faculty and administration support. This doesn't mean you can't take steps to encourage support. Invite the faculty to attend your swim meets, or ask them to be timers to get them involved. Sometimes it's best when the invitation to attend or to time meets comes from team members, because teachers, principals, and athletic directors are usually flattered that their attendance means so much to the swimmers.

I expected our high school swimmers to be leaders in school, and the faculty knew I would cooperate fully in seeing to it that all team members met their academic requirements. Coaches need to check in and communicate often with teachers. The team and I also served the school in areas outside of swimming, cooperating in many faculty and administration projects when we could. We sold tickets to various school activities, sold Christmas trees, raised funds through community dinners, and attended other athletic events as part of our volunteer school duties. All of these efforts produced for our swim team a special rapport with the faculty and administration.

One of our faculty members, to whom I gave some swim lessons, built our starting blocks, weight benches, and even our bleachers. A shop teacher who swam with me made some of our first hand paddles and our water polo goals. As I described in chapter 2, many of our faculty and administration acted in several of our annual water shows. I didn't believe that we could get teachers into bathing suits for swimming and then into costumes for the out-of-water skits, but we did. It raised school morale and was great fun for both students and faculty.

As our successes in the pool increased, our swim team and even our high school received more recognition. Our school principal always accompanied our team when we were recognized and honored with various citations by such groups as the Washington State Senate, the Pierce County Commissioners, and the Tacoma City Council. Many community service clubs were also giving us special recognition each year. Placing several swimmers on the Olympic and other international swimming teams earned considerable community attention. Foreign teams and coaches coming to Tacoma for competition and training camps also helped us get noticed. All of this favorable attention, combined with our academic and volunteer efforts, secured great support from our high school faculty and administration.

Gaining Financial Support

The athletic budget is your base in a high school program, because it reflects the ability of your team to generate income, and we all know how difficult that can be in non-revenue sports such as swimming.

Nevertheless, you should try to create at least one major meet that can generate income. Our income event was the Ram Relays during the Christmas vacation, which became so successful for us that in some years it was named the homecoming event for our winter sports season. We assured ourselves a large crowd by selling a substantial number of tickets during the several weeks leading up to the event.

Because our student council was another potential source of money, I encouraged some swimmers to run for a position on the council. The student council advisor was usually a friend of the swim team and a star performer in our faculty water show. When we had a need to fund a pool project, our student council was a great ally.

For example, our student council funded the construction of bleachers to ensure adequate spectator seating. On another occasion, when the student council conducted a survey asking what school project was most needed that year, school officials were surprised that students voted for better acoustics for the swimming pool. The swim team's lobbying efforts paid off, because the student council appropriated

enough money to start the project, about $800 toward the total cost of $10,000. The faculty volunteered the labor to start the project. Because the issue had attracted so much attention, the school district finished the job. The high school budget is usually sufficient to cover at least the minimal requirements of travel, uniforms, and officials. Some supplemental fund-raising may be necessary to add something special for the team. Swim-a-thons, auctions, raffles, and special sales such as candy, Christmas trees, or old uniforms can bolster your funds.

Building a Club Program

I will discuss some methods for building a club program that distinctly differ from those for building a high school program. Club swimming should be enhanced by receiving new swimmers each year from the high school program.

Recruiting Swimmers

Every year I coached, I recruited new swimmers successfully from our Wilson High School team for Tacoma Swim Club. These were swimmers who were new to competitive high school swimming—first time swim team members. I wanted them to continue to improve, and the best method was to have them participate in a longer swim year. Their successful teammates who were already Tacoma Swim Club swimmers were the best recruiters.

In recruiting club swimmers, you should focus on a younger age-group. The high school swimmers who start swimming in high school are good candidates for a year-round swim club program. However, a successful swim club will need a continuous influx of younger swimmers. Community swimming classes are one of your best sources for finding new swimmers. You must recruit at every community pool that offers children's swim classes, from the local YMCA to your city park district program. You should also try the summer swim leagues in your area.

Club Entry Levels

New club swimmers must be able to enter at some level of your club at any time during the year. Your club should have a minimum-swimming-proficiency test for candidates, and those who pass can be placed into one of the team levels. Swimmers not yet able to pass the test should be placed into advanced swim classes somewhere in the community program and called back for a second test after an appropriate period of time.

I've found that a tiered system of ranking swimmers works best in training and goal-setting. I have a three-level system for my age-group swimmers and two additional levels for my older and more advanced swimmers. This is an ability-level grouping that challenges all swimmers without placing them in a program over their heads.

Level I is the entry level for young, new swimmers and is designed to maintain for them an exciting, energetic challenge. Most of all, this level must be fun, so we emphasize games and relays at the practice sessions. For example, when they're in the pool you can have them play water tag; out of the water, you can have such games as costume contests on Halloween.

A high percentage of your practice sessions must be devoted to instruction. Your swimmers need to be taught the basic skills, including the fundamental technique drills in all four competitive swim strokes, the streamlined or "torpedo" position off each wall, the basic turn skills, and streamlined kicking skills.

You should teach Level I swimmers the proper use of the pace clock. Swimmers need to know how to read it, and how to maintain the designated spread (in seconds) between swimmers in their lane. Your swimmers must also develop the discipline of starting and finishing at the wall and adhering to the team-established circle patterns within a lane. My Level I swimmers usually come from the 10-and-under age-group and I call them our novice team.

Level II is the intermediate step in your age-group program. Swimmers in this level do more endurance-type games, some social events, and some team yells for competition. The relay games you would have them participate in would be longer and more continuous than those of the first level. Social events would include special pool activities on Halloween, Christmas, and Valentine's Day. Teach them team yells for the start of their competition at swim meets. My second-level swimmers learn some Tacoma Swim Club team yells.

Your instruction of intermediate swimmers involves advanced turns and stroke drills, basic race strategies, awareness of stroke count, and some basic video analysis. Teach them how to pass swimmers in the lane and how to be the lead swimmer. Also instill in them the necessity of reporting to practice on time. Level II swimmers are usually 9 to 12 years old and are called AA swimmers in our program.

Level III is the advanced competitive level in your age-group program, and is designed to become more goal-oriented. Quality instruction is crucial at this level. Your swimmers must become very proficient in their technique in all four competitive strokes. The prime event in this age-group should be the 200-yd individual medley. You need to add more strength and flexibility training at this level. Also, you should emphasize the importance of sleep, nutrition, and a healthy athletic lifestyle, and if you haven't already addressed it, discuss the detrimental effects of recreational drug use. The swimmers in Level III are usually 11 to 14 years old, and we classify them as AAA.

You'll need to add a level or two in order for your club to succeed beyond age-group swimming. Tacoma Swim Club has two additional levels beyond age-group, both of which are in the senior program. The first of these, the prenational level, is open to all swimmers who are within a specified number of seconds of the senior regional time standards; the other, the national training group, is for those swimmers who have attained the senior regional time standards. I have swimmers age 12 and up in these two groups. Performance is the chief criterion for entry at this level.

The prenational training team members are slower swimmers than our national training group, but both groups train to improve their endurance levels and to prepare for their major event, the 400-yd individual medley. Having the same major event assures that these swimmers will continue to train in all four competitive strokes. Here your primary job is quality control. You must emphasize good stroke technique and training habits in order to develop swimmers' speed and endurance, two important components at both of these training levels.

Your requirements for these levels may change slightly depending on the abilities of your current team members. You may need more levels or fewer, but this tiered system, which serves as the basis for our club program, permits movement toward more challenging levels for every team member.

Gaining Financial Support

Each club must raise the money required to meet their yearly budget, including the money necessary to rent pool time, to pay the coaches, and to cover the expenses of uniforms, travel, and competition.

I started Tacoma Swim Club on a shoestring. We didn't have a budget. I volunteered to coach without pay. Fortunately, we had free pool space at the time.

Within a couple of years, however, we had developed a parent booster club, composed of a fund-raising chairperson, a treasurer, and other officers who would ensure our club's financial stability.

Monthly or quarterly swimmer fees usually form the base of the pyramid in club fund-raising. Other sources of revenue come from a variety of projects, such as swim meets, clinics, camps, and all of the methods previously listed. If you can recognize and accept your needs, you can find a person in your club with the talents to raise the necessary funds.

Community service clubs have been very helpful to us on occasion with special funding. In addition, the city park department, local YMCAs, schools, or other community organizations will often cooperate with the local swim club by providing pool time at minimal or no cost.

Alumni can also play a major role in fundraising. Though we have not yet organized our available alumni support, we do have several alumni who have initiated donations to our club. We now receive about $4,000 a year in alumni donations.

Masters swimming is another good way to generate revenue. Providing the time and space for the older swimmers who still compete can be profitable, because they can afford to pay club fees and usually know how to raise money in their community. Pool availability has limited my club team from developing a masters level, but I hope to be able to include them before the end of my

coaching career, because their support can be beneficial to the club and to themselves.

Whenever we really wanted or needed something, we raised the money. One year we needed money to send our team on an exchange to Norway and Wales, so we conducted a fund-raiser that quickly earned $12,000. Another year we decided to purchase automatic timing for a 10-lane pool. Again, we raised about $12,000 through community service clubs and foundation grants.

  A GOAL TO EUROPE

The year we raised $12,000 for our first trip to Europe, I set goals for every team member. Every swimmer who achieved the minimum-dollar goal qualified for a two-day bus trip across the state. On the first day we competed in a swim meet, and on the second, we went to the World's Fair in Spokane. Two busloads totaling almost 100 members earned the trip, which was a great majority of our total team.

We have taken our club team to Europe three times for competition. We have also traveled to Mexico, Puerto Rico, and the Virgin Islands. All of these occasions required additional financial support, so don't get discouraged. When there is the will, there is a way. Don't use lack of funds as an excuse for having a second-rate swim club, because every team has the ability to attain the necessary financial support.

Similar Issues

I have explored the major contrasts in high school and club swimming in this chapter, and now I would like to examine the similar areas of building a swimming program.

Establishing Fan Support

Fan support is easier to establish in a high school program than it is in a club. For one thing, a high school swim meet lasts about 1-1/2 hrs, and when you win in a high school setting, you're going to attract fans who have some association with the school and community, not just swimmers' parents. As the media announced our unbeaten high school record of 40, 50, 100, 200, and 300 meets, our fan attendance rose accordingly.

STAR ATTRACTION

When we had a potential American record holder in Kaye Hall at our high school, we would hold special events for her. Kaye was in high school before we had a competitive swim team for the girls, so on occasion, we would have Kaye conduct an attempt at the American record during a boys' high school swim meet. The proper sanctions and the necessary officials were arranged for the event at a time when it was within the rules. In these special swims, Kaye produced at least two American records, and again fans were showing up at our swim meets in increasing numbers.

A word of caution: Don't set up a special event like this unless you are quite certain that it can be done. Though you can gain credibility quickly by doing what you have set out to do, you can lose it even faster by failing. In my case, both Kaye and I were certain she would break the record as she had almost done it in a regular practice session.

The more fans who show up for swimming meets the better. People attract people, and numbers attract greater numbers. When we first opened Wilson High School, I used to do anything to get fans in the bleachers. I gave students in my physical education classes extra credit for attending swim meets, and I brought in the pep band to play at the competition.

The pep band always helped create excitement. I would suggest you arrange pep buses to travel to your state meet, because when you fill pep buses, and bring your pep band, you are assured of a strong fan base at the championship.

Creating fan support for club swimming is more challenging. Most meets are much longer and can go all day. Parents, relatives, and close friends make up most of the fan support at these meets. Their support is very important, and you must actively encourage it. Arranging a special seating section for your team's parents and friends will make it more of a social setting for them and will simultaneously focus the placement of your fan support.

In addition to the fans in attendance, media attention can generate fan support and provide a firm support base. However, remember that to get media attention, you have to make an effort to report swim meet results and to nurture relationships with local media members.

Making the Program Visible

Naturally, a winning program that produces individual state, American, world, and Olympic record holders is going to get attention. However, in my case, it didn't start out this way.

In my first year of coaching at Lincoln High School, I faced an uphill battle. The team had been on the losing end for several years. We needed to turn that around to attract any attention, so in our first year we moved up to third place at the state championship, and in our second we tied at state for first place.

We didn't talk about state records in those early years; instead, we went after what was attainable. We listed our school's varsity records and sought to break them. The record times were not fast for the most part, but the media nevertheless reported each record-breaking performance. This brought our swim team to the attention of our high school and gradually to our community.

Our second step to gain visibility was to defeat our cross-town rivals, who were the current state champions. When Lincoln High School, after only my second year of coaching, defeated Stadium High School of Tacoma in two very close dual meets, the entire community began to notice our swim program.

When Wilson High School was built, we had everything in place. Because it was a new school, almost every swim set a new varsity record. Then we started to break almost every state record, and we continued to do this year after year until I retired from coaching high school swimming. We also began an incredible unbeaten streak for all high school swim meets that lasted 24 years.

Our swimmers, both in club and in high school, broke national high school, American, Olympic, and world records. The high school team's list of All-American swimmers continued to grow, while the Tacoma Swim Club swimmers were being recognized with world ranking more frequently. Visibility was never a problem after the first few years.

Instilling Pride in the Team

Pride comes from your swimmers' accepting the discipline necessary for team success. The discipline that builds this pride is reflected in the team's work ethic.

Regardless of the difficulty in doing so, some of your swimmers' bad habits have to be changed and replaced with good ones. Successful swimming is the result of a great amount of hard work over an extended period of time. Swim team members must understand the necessary level of training intensity required for success, and then they must commit to attaining that intense training level. Pride comes from the completion of such challenging training sets. Pride also comes when their teammates challenge them to be faster in these training sets.

You will find that your swimmers who have paid the price for personal success, who have completed the most intensive sessions in their training, will have a very high level of personal pride, as well as a very high athletic fitness level.

Team pride results from individual pride. The team that works together, plays together, and competes together becomes like a family. When every member discovers the pride that comes from committing to intensive training, then they are prepared to compete with confidence.

Cheering

When your swimmers cheer for one another, it builds pride and cohesiveness in the team. Your swimmers will produce an even greater effort when their teammates show their appreciation.

The results of cheering are obvious during swim-offs. When two or more swimmers have the same times for the last available position in the championship or consolation final, they "swim off" for that remaining available position. When the entire team stands at the sides and ends of the pool, cheering for their teammate to win, it has a great impact on the results of the race.

I always tell my swimmers that I can't remember when one of our team members has ever lost a swim-off. I also tell them that even though this may be a slight stretch of the truth, I expect them nevertheless to reach down for something extra. We usually do win our swim-offs, but even when we lose, we build pride in our team by going down with a fight.

Winning Close Races

Winning close races also builds pride. Anytime we are close in a race, we want to be the toughest and strongest of all the swimmers coming to the finish line. Always recognize your swimmers who manage to beat an opponent in a close race, whether it's for first place, or for second or third.

Relays

One indication of team pride occurs when your swimmers' times are better in relays than they are in individual events. Swimmers should be as good or better in a relay position than they are in their individual events for the same distance. Pride develops when all relay team members contribute to the effort at no less than their personal-best individual swim.

Tradition

Finally, team pride comes from tradition. I posted an honor roll for every swimming event at our high school; it was printed on a kickboard bearing the name, the year, and the time listed for each swimmer who attained the specified honor roll time. We also listed all of our varsity and state records, and our All-Americans on special display boards.

Pride comes from swimming faster in both the prelims and finals; it comes from a great performance, be it winning or swimming a new personal-best time; finally, it is a necessary ingredient in personal success and is vital to team success. Our Wilson High School swimmers have said that it meant something special to compete in a Wilson team uniform. Such pride can be instilled in every athlete and team, and the opportunities to do it are always present. You and your athletes have to learn to recognize and to use those opportunities to build team pride.

Summary

Building a swim program requires a well-organized plan with specific goals. In this chapter, I explained the keys to successful high school and club swim programs:

1. Swimmers who are good students and citizens will build faculty and administration support.
2. Coaches and swimmers serving their school outside of competition will assure the support of the faculty and administrators.
3. Recruit the best potential swimmers within your high school.
4. Establish an age-group swim team to provide a strong base of swimmers for your high school teams.
5. Provide training and competitive levels for all participants on your high school team.
6. Develop and encourage extensive fund-raising activities for your club swimming program.
7. Make your club team accessible to new swimmers year-round, providing enough levels to challenge all team members.
8. Incorporate fun, instruction, and discipline into your program.
9. Build fan support from your team's successes.
10. Develop team pride by helping your swimmers develop the discipline that comes with intensive work habits.
11. Use victories in swim-offs, relays, and close races to build your team's pride.

Part II

Coaching Plans

Chapter 5

Planning for the Season

I believe in the old maxim that "The failure to plan is the same as planning to fail." I always began planning for the next high school season within a few days after a state championship meet.

Every year that I have coached, I have tried to live by the philosophy, "To be satisfied is to be finished." As I have stated, for me, planning always starts soon after concluding even a very successful state championship meet, because at that time, everything is in its proper perspective to evaluate the past season and begin to plan for the next. I always ask myself, "What went well and what went wrong?"

Developing Your Plan

A well-written plan will chart your course for the coming year or longer. Your swim-

mers commit more readily to a long-range plan when they see it written. Planning allows me to commit myself to my best effort over any given time period.

The Planning Time Period

The time period for which you plan can be for the few months of a short high school season, for the full year, or for even a longer period of time. Typically, for the most success, you should plan for the full school year as a high school coach. I always had two plans, a general one that extended through each athlete's entire high school career and a specific one for each full year.

As a club coach, I also plan for one full year. Club coaches will have a minimum of two competitive seasons, the short course and the long course seasons, within a year. Short course, usually in the fall and winter, is in 25-yd and 25-m pools. Long course, in the spring and summer, is in 50-m pools.

Many club coaches will plan for the three-season year. The third season occurs in fall and has a championship meet designed to attain the time standards necessary to enter the championship meets of the short and long course seasons, which come later in the year.

A quadrennial, or 4-year, plan is designed to lead into each Olympic Games. National teams and some elite athletes will train under a quadrennial plan specifically in order to reach their peak performance level for the Olympic Games.

The Ingredients of a Plan

Your plan should include preseason conditioning, the competitive season, the postseason transition, and the breaks.

Preseason planning would include these elements:

1. The dryland cross-training necessary to attain the highest level of physical fitness by the start of the swim training
2. The gradual increases in distance and intensity of the swimming to assure adaptation
3. The basic technique skills that require special emphasis
4. The motivational methods that will best achieve the endurance-swimming base necessary for later success in competition
5. The amount and frequency of the speed work

The competitive season would include the following:

1. The maintenance of sufficient training during the regular season competition
2. The special drills for starts, turns, finishes, and relay exchanges
3. The amount and frequency of speed and endurance training
4. The amount of rest, if any, that will be necessary for any of the regular season meets

Planning considerations for the postseason transition are these:

1. An evaluation of the season and of each swimmer

2. A determination of the amount of dryland cross-training
3. The preparation necessary for the next season and how best to accomplish it
4. The length of time away from water training

Planning breaks would include these factors:

1. The amount and intensity of training that will be expected during final exams
2. The training schedule on the holidays
3. The maintenance of the high levels of physical fitness during any extended holiday periods

You should plan the transition from high school swimming to club swimming when you are the high school coach, including your encouragement of your high school swimmers to report to their club coach as soon as possible after their high school season. You should provide the club coach with your swimmers' best training times and their championship meet results.

Similarly, when you are the club coach, you should plan the transition from club swimming to high school swimming. You need to work out a training plan with the high school coach. Your swimmers may continue to swim some club meets during the high school season, depending on the interscholastic rules in their state. As club coach you've likely known your swimmers for an extended period of time, so inform the high school coach about their best events, their training habits, and whatever else can help ease the transition.

As a club coach, you need to recognize the great value of high school swimming. Your swimmers have a good opportunity to excel on a high school team, because the competition is spread a little thinner over more high school teams. Also, high school sports receive more media coverage, so good swimmers get recognized. High school swimming also places a special emphasis on speed, which can help develop your swimmers in that important area.

On the other hand, if you're a high school coach, you should recognize that club swimming provides year-round training opportunities and places a premium on multiple distances. Emphasis on more events and longer distances in all strokes in club swimming make the club swimmer the nucleus of a successful high school team.

 A STATISTICAL FACT

With a few exceptions, the swimmers who win and place at the state high school championship meets are almost always year-round swimmers with club experience. I had individual event high school state champions who had not been club members prior to high school, but they became year-round swimmers in order to win. This is a fact in swimming, so you should plan accordingly.

The Master Calendar

Make out a master calendar and list your schedule of competition as the first step (see Figure 5.1). Build everything else around this meet schedule.

Which meets are important and how important? Which is the most significant meet that your team will enter during that season? It was always the state championship meet for our Wilson High School team that determined the success of our team.

The U.S. Swimming Senior National Championship meet would ideally be the most significant meet for our Tacoma Swim Club. Every fourth year the Olympic Trials would ideally become our most important competition.

For grass-roots swim clubs, the meet most important would likely be a championship meet prior to the Senior National Championship, because the great majority of clubs are developing and are not large swim centers. Most beginning clubs will have too few swimmers who qualify for a Senior National Championship to make a legitimate run at winning at that level.

 ONLY THE ELITE QUALIFY

Tacoma Swim Club has had many swimmers score at the Senior National Championship meet, and we placed teams in the top ten several times. However, the number of qualifiers for the national championship is usually small. The size of our national team entry has varied from 1 to a high of 21. The average size of those teams qualifying to attend the Senior National Championship is only two or three swimmers, which is too few for a significant team finish.

Our most important team championship will more often be the association, region, zone, or Junior National Championship meet.

You should indicate which meets are important enough to require some rest and designate which swimmers on the team should rest. Stress the importance of the state championship meet as the culmination of all your efforts in previous competitions. Here is where your swimmers should give their best performances.

November 1—All required forms completed and turned in to the athletic director.

November 7—First day of swim practice.

November 24—Intrasquad meet and school dismissed for Thanksgiving holidays.

December 6—Dual meet.

December 9—Dual meet.

December 13—Dual meet.

December 16—Dual meet.

December 20—Dual meet.

December 23—School dismissed for semester break.

January 3—School resumes.

January 6—Dual meet.

January 13—*Dual meet: a major city rival.*(No rest but a special effort.)

January 16—Martin Luther King Jr. holiday.

January 20—Dual meet.

January 27—Dual meet.

February 4—*District championship meet.*(Taper, rest, and shave only for the non–state meet qualifiers.)

February 17, 18—***State championship meet.***(Taper, rest, and shave for all state meet participants.)

Figure 5.1 A sample master calendar for high school.

Listing your competitive schedule is a first step. You can add the daily training sessions and the vacation training schedule to a monthly plan (see Figure 5.2) that is more inclusive. List the major school functions, such as formal dances and the semester final exam days as well, because you need to know when the academic pressure is the greatest on your swimmers.

A FOREIGN EXAMPLE

I had a close friend, Dave Haller, who was the national coach for Hong Kong. He was from Great Britain, and most of his swimmers were from Chinese families. He soon became aware of the cultural differences of his Hong Kong swimmers. For one thing, his swimmers would cease to come to practice for about 3 weeks during final exam time. Dave soon learned that they made classwork their Number 1 priority, and he planned accordingly after his first year.

Planning the Season Training Schedule

Planning for the season must include training. My training plan provides for a cycle of varying stress or intensity levels. You can permit recovery and adaptation between training loads within your cycle. Table 5.1 shows my 15-week plan for a typical high school season. High school swimmers must be in good aerobic condition at the start of the season to attain the most success in this plan.

My plan allows for three cycles lasting 4 weeks each. Cycle 1 would be endurance; Cycle 2 would be endurance and quality; and Cycle 3 would be endurance, quality, and maintenance. The final three weeks are de-voted to peak preparation. (Because my club season is considerably longer than 15 weeks, I schedule a minimum of 8 weeks of endurance training for my minimum base.)

When developing your training schedule, your plan must assure that all levels of training intensity are provided at appropriate periods within each week throughout the season. This is the cycle that you build into your training calendar. Insert drills—kicking, pulling, starts, turns, finishes, relay exchanges, and whatever else you believe is necessary within this intensity guideline. The process of preparing individual workouts is outlined in chapter 6. When planning distances, adjust your yardage goals to accommodate the pool time available, the specific event needs, and the swimming background of each team member.

The cycle of varying intensities I first used in 1974 is different from what I am using now. Changing your plan from season to season is necessary, because swimming science may provide new information from current and ongoing research. Your own experience will cause you to review your plan at the end of each season. I vary my team practice plans according to which stage of the season (early, mid, or late) we're in.

Early Season

The main emphasis in the early season must be endurance training. Your endurance base is your foundation for sustained racing speed later in the season when you will need it most.

The intensity of your training sets is less demanding in the early season. Training distances are longer and the rest intervals are short in endurance training. I like to build

---

Training schedule: December 1–23—Monday, Wednesday, and Friday training at 5:30 a.m.; Monday through Friday training at 2:45 p.m.; Saturday training at 8 a.m.
December 24–31—Monday through Saturday training at 8 a.m. and 2 p.m. (Christmas off.)

Team meetings: December 6—Our team approach to the dual meet season: uniform, team seating, teammate support, event selection, premeet warm-up, and postmeet training. December 12—Review the holiday training schedule and the goals for that training opportunity. December 26—Motivational report from one or more of our returning college swimmers.

Special events: December 2—Goal and split times due. December 24—The Christmas Eve special training session with games and gifts. Week of December 26—one-on-one swimmer/coach conferences with all team members. Plan when and where your most intense training can best fit into this master calendar. Plan when and where the rest and the peak preparation will come.

Figure 5.2 A sample season plan for high school.

Table 5.1 Fifteen-Week Plan for a Typical High School Season

	Monday	Tuesday	Wednesday	Thursday	Friday	Saturday
Week 1						
A.M.	EN1	Off	EN1	Off	EN1	EN2
P.M.	EN1	EN1	EN2	EN1	EN1/SP3	Off
Week 2						
A.M.	EN1	Off	EN1	Off	EN1	EN1/SP3
P.M.	EN2/SP3	EN1/SP3	EN2/SP3	EN1/SP3	EN2/SP3	Off
Week 3						
A.M.	EN1	Off	EN1	Off	EN1/SP3	EN2/SP3
P.M.	EN2/SP3	EN1/SP3	EN2/SP3	EN3	EN1/SP3	Off
Week 4						
A.M.	EN1/SP3	Off	EN1	Off	EN1/SP3	EN2/SP3
P.M.	EN2/SP3	EN3/SP3	EN2/SP3	EN1/SP3	EN2/SP3	Off
Week 5						
A.M.	EN1/SP3	Off	EN1/SP3	Off	EN1	EN2/SP3
P.M.	SP1/EN1	EN3/SP3	EN1/SP3	EN2/SP3	SP1/SP3	Off
Week 6						
A.M.	EN1/SP3	Off	EN1	Off	EN2	EN2/SP3
P.M.	SP2/EN1	EN2/SP3	EN1/SP3	EN3	SP1/SP3	Off
Week 7						
A.M.	EN1/SP3	Off	EN1	Off	EN1/SP3	EN2/SP3
P.M.	SP1/EN1	EN2/SP3	EN3/SP3	EN1/SP3	SP2/EN1	Off
Week 8						
A.M.	EN1/SP3	Off	EN1	Off	EN1/SP3	EN3/SP3
P.M.	SP2/EN1	EN2/SP3	EN3/SP3	EN1/EN2	SP1/EN1	Off
Week 9						
A.M.	EN1/SP3	Off	EN1	Off	EN1/SP3	EN2/SP3
P.M.	SP1/EN1	EN2/SP3	EN3/SP3	EN1/EN2	SP2/EN1	Off
Week 10						
A.M.	EN1	Off	EN1/SP3	Off	EN1/SP3	EN2/SP3
P.M.	EN3/SP3	SP2/SP3	EN2/EN1	EN1/SP3	SP1/EN1	Off
Week 11						
A.M.	EN1	Off	EN1/SP3	Off	EN1/SP3	EN3/EN1/SP3
P.M.	SP2/SP3	EN2/EN1	EN1/SP3	SP1/EN1	SP2/EN1	Off
Week 12						
A.M.	EN1	Off	EN1	Off	EN1/SP3	EN3/EN1/SP3
P.M.	SP2/SP3	EN2/SP3	SP1/SP3	EN3/SP3	SP2/EN1	Off

Weeks 13-15

(Peak preparation or taper period—see chapter 11.)

Key: Training categories—United States Swimming, Sports Science Committee

System Symbol	Pulse Rate	Work/Rest Ratio	% Velocity
REC[1]	Up to 120	Choice	80% Threshold Speed
EN1	120–140	10–30 seconds rest	95% Threshold Speed
EN2	130–170	10–30 seconds rest	Threshold Endurance Speed
EN3	160–180	20 seconds rest to 1:1	107% Threshold Speed
SP1	Max	1:1 to 1:2	Inside 90% Max Velocity
SP2	Max	1:2 to 1:8	Inside 95% Max Velocity
SP3[2]	Max	1:2	100% to 110% Max Velocity

[1]REC is used where appropriate in my training but is not listed as a major emphasis on my season plan. There are gray areas or categories that overlap. The listed daily training categories on my high school season plan indicate which training categories received the most importance at each training session.

[2]SP3 refers to very short speed efforts over 10 to 25 yards.

into long kicking sets during the endurance buildup.

Endurance 2, or anaerobic threshold swimming, provides the most intensive sets in this early period. Anaerobic training is seldom used during this phase. Speed work over very short distances should be used to maintain and build speed throughout the season. Remember to teach correct technique throughout this training. Adhere to the skills and drills that will be your model through the complete season.

Midseason

You should begin to train your swimmers anaerobically with speed 1 and 2 after the early season endurance phase has been completed. Specific race-pace training must be included at this time. You will maintain your swimmers' endurance through aerobic swimming but less frequently than you did in the early season. Endurance 2 sets are reduced slightly but still used about twice a week to maintain a good endurance base.

Throughout midseason you should continue the short sets of speed work over very short distances. Focus frequently on starts, turns, finishes, and relay exchanges during this period.

Late Season

Late-season training is your final phase before starting the peak preparation for the final championship meets. Speed training will reach its peak during this stage of the training season, but you should also continue some endurance training to maintain your swimmers' good endurance base.

Late season is also a time to sharpen your swimmers. Swimming at race-pace should be precise and on target; everything must begin to come together.

Peak-preparation training will be explained in chapter 12.

Getting Ready Physically

Preparing your swimmers is the key to a successful championship performance. My goal is to get our new high school swimmers into a very high level of physical fitness as

soon as possible. Once they attain that high level, they should strive to reach even *higher* fitness levels. Your high school swimmers must reach and maintain great fitness in order to continue improving in the program; there is no going back or standing still in this matter.

Our club program is designed to gradually develop in swimmers higher levels of physical fitness throughout their swimming careers. Competitive swimmers are often recognized as the most fit students, even in elementary school. Such benefits are the result of their year-round swimming programs. In my experience, students who swim score higher on tests for both strength and endurance than those who don't.

The seasonal concept in high school sports promotes the idea that you can get into physical condition in the few weeks of the high school season. Nothing could be further from the truth. High school swimmers must be at an elevated level of personal physical fitness at the start of the swim season to be successful.

I call my idea the "total-athlete" concept. Each swimmer must train to be a complete athlete, meaning that she or he must get into top condition and remain there as a minimum level.

Progressive total fitness can make the difference between a good swimmer and a great one. Patient and continuous physical preparation is necessary. The "physical machine" that each swimmer brings to the starting blocks each year must be fitter and better than in the previous year. However, remember that this is a continuous and gradual process. Don't expect to make a significant difference in a short period of time.

 FITTER IS FASTER

When I formed the total-athlete concept, I soon discovered many great examples of continuous improvement in my program. Janet Buchan, one of my average ninth-grade swimmers, continued to improve physically each year through diligent training and broke state high school records during her final 2 years at Wilson High School and continued as a collegiate champion at Stanford University. Susan Lenth and Dana Powers, two of my swimmers from Tacoma Swim Club, also raised their fitness levels through each year, swimming their best times ever in their senior year of college.

We can make the difference by our teaching and our example. Personal fitness is not a sometime thing but a goal worthy for a lifetime. We need to provide programs of strength training and flexibility exercises throughout the year. Our ability to measure the results of our training will provide more motivation for the swimmers.

Transition-Training

Swimmers have a break at the end of the summer season, which may be from 2 up to 6 weeks. There will be another break after the short course winter season, usually during the school spring vacation. This swimming break should be short, 1 week or less, but it may extend to a longer time period. During these breaks in their training, swimmers can lose strength and endurance rapidly.

The best solution to maintain fitness-levels through breaks is cross-training, or what I call transition-training. Swimming, in itself, won't prepare swimmers to be the best that they can be. Cross-training is necessary to maximize strength and to develop flexibility. My transition-training minimizes swimming, though it would be best if the athlete continued to do some swimming at reduced distances and on fewer days. We even take a complete break from swimming for the shorter time periods to provide a better mental adjustment for the next swimming start.

However, I always continue our basics of 300 sit-ups and 100 push-ups each day. Jogging, running hills, biking, circuits, strength-training, and even triathlons have all played a part in our transition-training. Whatever you choose, try to provide something new in your swimmers' exercise program to ignite their interest level. Swimmers should improve their fitness base and their percent body fat levels during these swimming breaks.

Strength

I believe the core, particularly the abdominal area, of the body must be very strong. The ability of a swimmer to rotate quickly from side to side is most important. Our daily sit-ups contribute to this core strength, as well as our use of medicine balls.

Strength in the extremities is also important, and should be built through weight training, swim benches, swim sleds, medi-cine ball exercises, and surgical tubing units in the dryland training. Provide 30 to 60 min daily for strength and flexibility training in addition to the swimming. Dryland strength equipment and sample dryland programs will be discussed in chapter 6.

Planning the Essentials

Each prospective swimmer must fulfill a number of preliminary requirements in order to join the swim team. I consider these requirements to be in the preplanning stage.

The high school swimmer usually must provide

1. results of a medical screening,
2. proof of insurance,
3. evidence of their student activity membership, and
4. a completed parental permission form.

The high school athletic director will often assume the responsibility of making sure your swimmers meet these requirements. Make sure that your athletes meet their responsibilities before the first scheduled practice.

Our Tacoma Swim Club registration chairperson assumes this responsibility for my club swimmers. Each family must complete a medical form, register in U.S. swimming, and become a club member in order to be a participant. Though I like to make certain each swimmer is channeled into the process, I prefer to have someone else specialize in completing this procedure.

Facilities and Pool Set-Up

Although you will not be able to make many changes in the structure of your training pool, you can change the pool environment in order to make it conducive to competitiveness.

 A NOTABLE EXCEPTION

Tacoma Swim Club actually changed the length of our city outdoor pool. Titlow Pool, 55 yd long for 39 years, was changed to 50 m. An additional concrete wall of about 12 in was added to the shallow end of the pool to make this possible. All of the materials were donated, and our club members volunteered the labor. We now have our needed regulation 50-m long course pool.

Your pool's water level can be maintained at the gutter to assure that it's relatively smooth. You can best coach stroke technique in a pool with a calm water surface. For this reason, your pool should also have turbulence-control lane lines. Make sure you can put them in and remove them quickly for swim team practice.

There's a great deal of other equipment you'll need to begin your practices. Backstroke flags must be in place at every training session, so your backstroke swimmers and individual-medley swimmers can practice all of their turns effectively and legally. Bulletin boards, white boards, and chalk boards must also be available for announcements and posting the day's training session for your swimmers.

I always had special interest display boards at Wilson High School, with one section containing a list of All-American swimmers from our school and another listing all of the Wilson High School state individual and relay event champions. I also had a special section for every high school team that won a state championship. Our team records board was a large 4 ft x 8 ft with large letters to print the names of our swimmers who held records.

A very special section to our swimmers was the honor roll boards. Each swimming event had a special kickboard attached to the wall of the pool. In order to have their names placed on the honor roll board, the swimmers would have to meet or surpass the time standard for their respective events.

Finally we had two super boards placed above the honor roll boards. One board was for those athletes who attained the honor roll time in every event, and the other was for those who broke a national high school record.

Student Managers

Your high school swim team needs student managers. I have always had several of the brightest young students available to assist me each practice day.

The ability to time every swimmer whenever the need arises in practice is only possible when you have enough capable student managers. The records boards, the daily motivational point tables, and the bulletin board are all areas of responsibility for your student managers.

In swim meets, your student managers can take the split times and can keep the running score during the competitions. They can also handle many other responsibilities that may range from the placement of special equipment in the pool area for the competition to getting the meet results to the newspapers, radio, and television outlets.

Medical Care

During practice and competitions, Wilson High School had a trainer on duty in the gym and in the pool buildings. Because swimming is not a contact sport, medical support has not traditionally been at poolside.

Consequently, swim coaches must have CPR and first aid training at minimum. Club coaches now need Coaches' Safety Training through the Red Cross in order to coach in U.S. swimming. Whatever emergency training is required, the emphasis remains on accident prevention. A contingency plan to respond to a pool accident must be in place and should be reviewed and rehearsed each season. Post the emergency number at the nearest telephone along with the instructions that need to be relayed.

Nutrition and Weight Guidelines

"Invisible training," those habits of preparation that are hidden from the coach, refers to the nutrition, the amount of sleep, and the rest that a swimmer attains. Proper invisible training is vital for the success of your swim teams. Your swimmers can't recover quickly from one practice session to another without adequate sleep and rest and good nutrition.

 A TRUE STORY

One of our young high school swimmers was at a plateau, discouraged because he was training hard and swimming slower. I asked him when he usually went to bed. He said he was retiring somewhere between 11 p.m. and midnight, and then getting up at 5 a.m. He believed that this was the only way he could maintain his academic goals. I suggested that he organize his available study time and get to bed by 9:30 p.m. He agreed reluctantly, but within 2 weeks, he attained best-ever swims in his events. His training also improved dramatically and, to his relief, his academic achievements didn't suffer.

During school vacations, I encourage daily naps between the two training sessions. Most of our swimmers have learned to take advantage of this invisible training necessity.

In dealing with weight, you should avoid weighing swimmers as a team procedure, because many are especially sensitive to this issue, and eating disorders are a serious problem that can result from pressure about weight. Besides, weight is not the best indication of excess body fat. Your goal of an acceptable lean body mass for your swimmers will vary for each individual and will differ substantially in males and females.

Each season one of our parents, trained to measure skin folds with medical calipers, would measure the girls in the privacy of their own locker room and the boys in a secluded section of the pool. I am the only other person who would see the test results. Though this is an uncomfortable fact of swim training, you have to measure swimmers in order to determine if a change in their diet is warranted. Its purpose is no different from using a stop watch to measure swim results.

Your swimmers are to be concerned only with their own tests. No comparisons are to be made with other swimmers, because each test is a barometer for its swimmer only. Swimmers have found that when they switch to lower fat foods, they attain lower levels of fat on their skin fold tests.

 THE ULTIMATE SACRIFICE

One summer several of our young women voluntarily gave up ice cream. I found out about it only after their skin fold tests resulted in very significant drops in their body fat. I asked them what had happened and they told me they had made a number of dietary changes, including the ultimate sacrifice of giving up ice cream for the summer season.

Roster and Events

I accept every swimmer who can swim safely and has some technical proficiency in the competitive swimming strokes. Likewise, you shouldn't worry about accepting too many athletes. A few will always drop out when they realize the degree of discipline, of time, and of effort that is involved to be successful. You don't know which swimmers will commit to the program until you give them the opportunity.

Swimmers can always be assigned to events as your team needs become clear. I coach all of my swimmers as individual-medley swimmers in their early training, because it stresses all four strokes in my teaching and training. If you use this individual-medley training attitude, you will produce your specialists in time. Swimmers will also have the ability to fill in for any event when the need arises.

Summary

Plan for at least a full year and not just the length of the season. The following suggestions will set you on the proper course:

1. Consider all ingredients necessary in your plan.
2. Build your plan around your master calendar.
3. Plan your training schedule.
4. Understand the terminology for the training systems.
5. Remember to communicate.
6. Keep in mind that physical preparation and maintenance are essential for every team member.
7. Train your swimmers to develop their core strength.
8. Determine what dryland strength equipment is available.
9. Preplan to ensure that your swimmers complete the necessary paper work.
10. Remember that student managers are a necessity for a good program.
11. Stress to your swimmers the importance of invisible training—proper amounts of sleep, rest, and nutrition.
12. Begin your swimmers in individual-medley training, which will fill the gaps in the team roster.

Chapter 6

Preparing for Practices

After planning your season, it is almost time to begin practice. However, before swimmers take their first strokes, you need to prepare for the practice sessions by making well-developed plans that detail what will happen in practice, what kinds of training equipment to use and how to use them, how you will conduct practice, how you will train your team, and what exercises swimmers will perform to build and maintain fitness. This chapter outlines these considerations and others that you must make when preparing for practices.

Setting Up the Practice Schedule

Set up the practice schedule during those times when your pool is available and when the swimmers are not attending school.

For the most success, I schedule two training sessions per day on Mondays, Wednesdays, and Fridays during the school year and every day but Wednesdays and Saturdays during summer vacation. We train at least once a day, except on Sundays. Because swimmers train in a medium much different from the one in which they live, they need to spend as much time as possible in the water in order to develop a feel for it. Measure their time in the water by the length of the swimming year, the number of training sessions, and the swimmers' attendance. The amount of time you allot to your swimmers each day depends on the availability of the swimming facilities.

Because swimming is easier on the muscles and the joints than other sports (e.g., running), there is less risk of injuries. Consequently, you can do double workouts within each week when practical during the school year, with the exception of maybe early season and peak preparation periods. Also remember that stress levels are always higher when school is in session, so more double workout days are possible during the summer and vacation periods.

Length of Practice

During the school year, we train 1-1/2 hr before school on the days of our morning workouts. Our afternoon sessions are usually 2-1/2 to 3 hr including the meetings and dryland training. Normally I schedule one 3-1/2-hr practice on Saturday mornings. I make an exception to this in May and June when preparing for the long course season and add a second workout on Saturday afternoons for the last month of school to give our swimmers more opportunities to be better prepared for summer training sessions.

I schedule a 3-hr practice session each morning during the summer, including the dryland training in this period. I then schedule a 2-hr practice session in the afternoons, except for Wednesdays and Saturdays, which are for recovery. Sundays are not scheduled training days throughout the year.

Naturally you may have to alter your schedule according to the availability of the swimming pool.

 IDEAL LENGTH OF TRAINING VERSUS AVAILABILITY

Although you may likely have less time available than I have outlined in this chapter, utilize the pool space and the available time that you do have. Regardless of limitations you can always be successful when you take full advantage of your situation. Club coach Scott Kerr, of Eugene, Oregon, told me that he only had the pool for 80 min each day during the school year. Yet one of his swimmers, Rachel Joseph, won several events at the Olympic Sports Festival and a Senior National Championship backstroke title.

The Training Course

I train my swimmers primarily short course during the school year, because our available pools are 25 yd or 25 m. A long course 50-m pool is available over the break between semesters, and we take advantage of it. Long course training facilitates endurance training, but it is not often available. If you do not have a long course pool available when preparing

for long course competition, add to the distance of your repeat swims. For example, do 10 × 225 or 250, in place of 10 × 200.

During the long course summer season, we train in a 50-m pool six mornings each week. I schedule our afternoon workouts in a short course pool, because I believe that swimmers will maintain more speed and a faster stroking tempo in short course training.

Another option we have in our short course pools is the cross-pool course. During both the long and short course seasons, I train cross-pool almost daily to emphasize and maintain speed training. My cross-pool course is over a 35-ft or 45-ft course depending on the pool we are using, which is slightly less or more than half the length of a 25-yd pool. Swimmers do more turns in cross-pool training, and they can swim at very fast speeds with less effort because of the frequent push-offs from the walls. Training cross-pool is also a good quality control station, because you can communicate technique tips more frequently.

Assigning Lanes

The wall lanes, unless they are extra wide, should not be used by backstroke, butterfly, or breaststroke swimmers, because they need enough lane space to maintain good technique. Your swimmers can't learn their strokes if they are hitting or trying to avoid hitting the wall while swimming. Freestylers who swim the crawlstroke will not have this problem.

In a six-lane pool with narrow wall lanes, assign one wall lane for the sprint freestyle swimmers. Sprint freestylers are less of a distraction to other swimmers at one side of the pool, because they rest more in their sets, they move to our diving well for cross-pool swimming, and they go to the swim benches more often.

For similar reasons, place your breaststroke swimmers next to the sprint lane. Then you can use two lanes for the backstroke and butterfly swimmers, which will allow you to give them the same sendoff. Such an arrangement will leave two lanes for the nonsprint freestyle swimmers.

My example would place swimmers in the lanes as follows:
Lane 1: sprint freestyle
Lane 2: breaststroke
Lane 3: backstroke

Lane 4: butterfly
Lanes 5 and 6: middle distance and distance freestyle

Individual-medley swimmers would be placed in appropriate lanes for each day's stroke specialization. If you have more or less than six lanes, you can adjust your options accordingly.

Circle Patterns

I prefer placing lane lines in between every two lanes instead of every one. Using a line between every other lane saves us time in setting up the pool for practice and again at the end. My swimmers circle clockwise in the odd-numbered lanes and counterclockwise in the even-numbered (see Figure 6.1). This permits better opportunities to pass by crossing to another lane when necessary, and also reduces the risk of collisions.

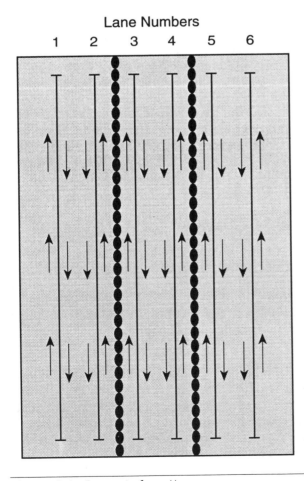

Figure 6.1 Lane circle patterns.

Training Equipment

I believe that to attain maximum success from your swimmers, you need training equipment. Equipment can duplicate the conditions of actual competition, enhance the teaching of stroke technique, and maximize the training effect.

Backstroke Flags

Have the backstroke flags in place every training session. Every backstroke swimmer must know the number of strokes necessary from the flags to the wall; if you practice with the flags in place, this becomes automatic. Flags are also necessary to minimize the risk of injury while turning.

Lane Lines

As I stated earlier in the chapter, I prefer placing lines between every two lanes for training sessions. Many coaches have every lane line in place for their practices. If you have wide lanes, this is an option; I, however, like to reserve this special effect for the day of competition.

Some days I don't put in any lane lines. The water then is choppy and swimmers do not feel as smooth as when the lines are in place. This makes the day of competition distinctive and gives the swimmer a unique psychological and physical effect.

Starting Blocks

Starting blocks must be in place at the deep end of the pool to meet safety standards. Use them for start and relay exchange practice during training. Don't permit swimmers to dive from the starting blocks unless you provide adequate supervision.

The major injuries in swimming usually result from diving accidents, including racing starts. Every U.S. swimming meet requires a feet-first entry with one hand on the pool deck by each swimmer entering the water for warm-up. Marshalls enforce the rule and monitor any designated racing start and sprint lanes during warm-up.

Pace Clocks

Pace clocks serve as assistant coaches and must be in place at every training session.

The clocks are used for send-off times, rest intervals, and the challenge of timing training swims.

Swimming Aids

I recommend using a number of swimming aids wherever they enhance your program. Some are more vital than others, and I will make that distinction. I have experimented with many training aids; I made hand paddles, underwater mirrors, and drag materials before they became commercially available.

Hand Paddles

I have long believed that paddles should be an aid for teaching above any other consideration. I designed my first paddles to enhance the swimmers' feel of the water and to increase their distance per stroke. When solid plastic paddles became available, I used them for many years, but I wasn't satisfied with their ability to improve stroke technique.

Consequently, I designed two new and unique hand paddles, Han's Paddles and the Gripper. Both paddles have holes to provide the feel of water on the hand. The holes also allow a faster stroking tempo than solid plastic paddles and present less risk of joint and muscle injury. The patented Gripper is an oversized holed paddle with a grooved tread on the water side.

Han's Paddle is a regular-sized paddle designed to improve technique and power. The Gripper is a technique paddle that maximizes the distance per stroke. Swimmers learn how to move their body past the stroking arm when using the Gripper.

My swimmers own both models, and we use them daily. I recommend both paddles to provide a change of water feel and to attain the most advantages from paddle swimming.

Swim Fins

Use a short swim fin for power kicking. More so than full-size fins, a shorter fin requires a more intense kick from the swimmer, with a range almost the same as in speed swimming.

A shorter fin contributes more to building power in the legs. You can either cut the regular-size fins shorter or you can now purchase short fins. I would finally suggest a softer shoe on the fin, because it is less irritating to the feet.

Rubber Bands

All of my swimmers have their own large rubber band to wear around their ankles when pulling. Rubber bands are good in all strokes, especially the backstroke. My swimmers keep the rubber band around their Han's Paddles and Grippers.

Goggles

Swim goggles are a must in training at every age-level. I can't believe that we used to train for hours without them. Goggles help your swimmers see better when judging the walls at turns, but mainly they help them avoid eye irritation from pool chemicals.

Tethered Swim Belts and Tubing

I use tethered swim belts and surgical tubing for tethered swimming. A short tubing with an attached belt need only be 6 to 12 ft in length to permit power kicking, pulling, or swimming to a tension point someplace within the pool. Longer tubing will permit both tethered swimming for the pool's full length and a speed-assisted return to the starting point.

Mirrors

I have used a wall mirror during almost all of my coaching career. The mirror serves as a technique coach for backstrokers. At deck level place a 5-1/2 to 6-1/2 ft mirror at the end wall of your pool. Angle the top of the mirror away from the wall so your swimmers can watch themselves swimming backstroke as they recede from the mirror.

Water Bottles

I require my swimmers, in order to avoid dehydration, to have their own water bottles to drink from during each training session.

Kickboards

I prefer kicking without kickboards, but we do use them for some of the sets. A smaller kickboard works better than those regular-sized, because it will usually permit your swimmers to kick at a body position close to that of actual swimming.

Pull Buoys and Inner Tubes

Pull buoys help streamline the lower body and hold it high enough in the water to simulate the position swimmers will have when moving fast. Use the smaller or medium-sized pull buoys for best results. Larger pull buoys lift most swimmers too high in the water and make training too easy. I do not use pull buoys extensively in my training program.

I sometimes use innertubes in my program to provide swimmers with added resistance when pulling. I prefer the 4-in. diameter innertubes. Innertubes can be used effectively with pull buoys to increase resistance while still retaining some of the advantages of the pull buoys. Backstrokers should not use pull buoys or innertubes, as I will explain in chapter 9.

Power Racks

Power racks are good for measuring and developing power in the water. You can measure your swimmers' improvement by the weight they can pull and the time they take to do a short swim. Sprinters love to work on the power rack.

However, the power rack is an expensive piece of equipment. Though I have one for our training, it is not vital if you cannot afford it; there are other equipment aids you can use to develop power, such as swimming with attached surgical tubing for resistance. Nevertheless, if you can afford it, the power rack is a great motivational tool and an effective aid for developing power.

Miscellaneous Aids

Many other aids should be used to evaluate your swimmers' effectiveness. For example, on occasion I will make conservative use of buckets that have attached surgical tubing and belts that connect to the swimmers' waists. Though I've not used them lately, drag suits also increase resistance while swimming. For some special training, I use soft divers' weight belts. Swimming with tennis shoes, shirts, or pants adds water resistance. A word of caution: Using any equipment that places the body in a position not conducive to fast swimming can be detrimental; you should always avoid using equipment that will have an adverse effect on technique.

Conducting Practice

Your practices must have a planned program, with your time carefully organized. You must have a time schedule that allows you to teach all of the skills that you deem necessary. You also need to systematically include a proper load—by load I mean the number of repeats, the distance to be swam, and the intensity of the swim—for all of the training systems (refer to Table 5.1). The proper load for your swimmers has to be built gradually to meet the needs of your team's ability-level.

Teach your swimmers flexibility exercises and have them stretch before they start each practice. Stretching gives swimmers some time to relax and talk before starting the water workout.

During the final minutes of their stretching, I usually go over with them the day's training plan, which is usually outlined on a whiteboard.

Components of a Practice

The warm-up is the same for all swimmers, and may be 800 to 1,200 yd or m long. I like to include some stroke drills in the warm-up to get the swimmers thinking technique early in the session. You should tailor your practices to fit your own style, choosing your components and their order in a manner that makes you comfortable.

I usually build into a kicking set soon after our warm-up. After the warm-up or the kicking set, I like some speed kicking cross-pool. Explosive swimming bursts come next while we are set up for cross-pool; I use the diving well, which is separate from the main pool, for these cross-pool speed bursts.

Lead into the main swimming set by doing maximum distance per stroke drills. Emphasizing special stroke technique prior to the main set can help your swimmers focus on good technique whenever they begin to feel fatigued through the full set of repeats.

Sculling and pulling are important components of your training session. Pulling refers to the normal armstroke used but without any kicking. Sculling is the hand and forearm motion used to press water by changing the pitch of the hand during the small out and in movement. I like using the paddles in most of the sculling and pulling. Grippers are excellent in the sculling.

Minimum number of strokes per length is an important training focus. As the season progresses, your swimmers need to train at race-pace and at the most efficient number of strokes to attain pace.

A specific-heart-rate set is a good method of clearing lactate at the end of practice; it provides a good warm-down and helps set up the recovery necessary between practices.

The great number of possibilities you can pursue to vary your sessions adds an exciting element to training. In any training session, you can stress any particular energy system or systems; there is no particular formula you have to or should have to use every day.

Review chapter 5 for the energy systems that you can utilize to keep your program exciting.

A sample practice session could include the components found in Table 6.1.

This sample workout, written into my training log before practice, shows my organized plan for the day. I present this plan only to illustrate my procedure, and I would not consider it appropriate for all situations; the energy system goal for each day, the ability-level of the swimmers, and the stage of the season would all impact my workout plan for any given day.

Dryland Training

Increasing your swimmers' strength and power can't be done as totally or as effectively in the water as it can in dryland training. Schedule a designated time for your dryland training when the equipment and facilities are available. Your time training out of the pool will also change during the course of the swim season according to the phase of your in-pool training. During the peak preparation period, your dryland training will decrease considerably; however, it will be at its highest point during transition training.

My dryland program changes every season according to my team's training phases and the availability of equipment and facilities. My dryland program includes the following: surgical tubing units, swim benches and swim sleds, medicine ball training, basic exercises, flexibility exercises, and weight training. However, I couldn't possibly utilize all of these on any one day because of time constraints and equipment availability. I would suggest rotating specific groups of swimmers through your planned dryland training on alternate days. Such an arrangement will result in the maximum use of the equipment you have available.

Surgical Tubing Units

Surgical tubing units are inexpensive and can be safely anchored to diving board railings and to wall eyebolts. I like to have them anchored at a position above shoulder height. Your swimmers, at minimal risk of injury to themselves, can duplicate swimming movements closely, resulting in an increased power and endurance that will transfer effectively to their swimming.

I use these units every season, and each swimmer owns their own. I prefer a paddle at each end of the tubing to simulate the hand position while swimming.

Table 6.1 Components of a Sample Practice Session

Set	Action	Training category (see p. 43)
Warm-up	400 free 200 back 200 back/free (alternating 5 strokes back, 5 strokes free with Han's Paddles)	REC
Kicking	3 × 200 (short fins) on 3 min (no kickboard, streamlined front lateral flutter kick)	EN1
Cross-pool explosive bursts	8 (4 × 15 or pool width) on 15 s. Kick on odd number (1, 3) underwater back butterfly in torpedo position. Swim even numbers (2, 4) in sprint butterfly. Rest 30 s between sets.	SP3
Stroke technique	3 × 100 with the Gripper on 1.5 min. Count strokes and hold the number of strokes for both 50s even on each swim.	EN1
Build set	3 × 100 on 1.5 min. Descend 1-3 to a heart rate count of 170.	
Main set	25 × 100 on a send-off that permits about 10 s rest. Maintain a heart rate of 170.	EN2 (Anaerobic threshold)
Recovery	Easy 200	REC
Sculling/pull set	12 ×100 on 1:40 min. (4 with the Gripper, 4 with Han's Paddles, 4 regular). Pull 75, scull 25 on the odd numbers; scull 25, pull 75 on the even numbers.	EN1

Here's a sample training session using a surgical tubing unit:

Perform each exercise for 30 repeats on one minute. Do the repeats of each exercise with fast movement but perfect technique. Perform three sets of each exercise in numerical order.

1. Butterfly pull-throughs
2. Elbow forward extension presses
3. Lateral forward arm swings
4. Butterfly recovery
5. Butterfly finish (second half of the stroke)
6. Butterfly pull-throughs (a second set)
7. Backstroke pull-downs
8. Breaststroke pull

One round of this particular set would take 24 min. The number of repeats and the rest interval would depend on the stage of the season. This particular set would probably fall in midseason. Remember to emphasize that each set must be with perfect technique and fast execution.

Swim Benches or Swim Sleds

Swim benches and swim sleds are both units on which the swimmers lie in a prone position and simulate a swimming stroke, usually butterfly. On the swim bench the body remains stationary, and the machine setting determines the amount of resistance that the armstroke will have to overcome. Swim benches can usually give you a power rating that is scored electronically.

On the swim sled swimmers lie on a moveable platform and pull their body past their arms, as they do in actual swimming. The swim bench helps the athlete attain the feeling of swimming while providing additional resistance. The body does not move past the arms on the bench, but your swimmers can duplicate fast swimming strokes with variable resistance.

Pair up your swimmers, with one doing the bench or sled exercises and the partner performing sit-ups, push-ups, or some other exercise while waiting. A typical sled set would be 5 × 20 repeats with good technique and a power pull on the sled. Partners would alternate on the sled after each set of 20. The swim bench set would vary the resistance and the number of repeats according to the stroke and distance swum.

Medicine Balls

I use rubber balls filled with water for inexpensive medicine balls. Regular medicine balls are not only expensive but they deteriorate more rapidly when they become wet. Medicine ball training increases core strength as well as that of the extremities. You should review a listing of recommended medicine ball exercises to determine which best serve your needs.

In using medicine balls, I like twist and turn drills, passing drills, and stomach exercises. You can create many interesting and motivational drills with medicine balls.

Basic Exercises

Our basic daily exercises include a minimum of 300 sit-ups and 100 push-ups, and when I have suitable equipment, I add pull-ups and dips to our program. The sit-ups and push-ups take very little time and can be done anywhere that is convenient to the swimmer.

Flexibility Exercises Provide your swimmers some time for flexibility exercises before they go into the water. At the Australian Institute of Sport, where a specialist teaches flexibility exercises at the start of each session, the swimmers report to practice 15 min early to do their exercises.

You must sell your swimmers on the benefits of being flexible. Teach them the necessary exercises at the start of the season. There are a number of excellent sources for flexibility exercises, including a booklet published by U.S. Swimming.

Weight Training Weight training has been an area of controversy for swimmers, because it is a form of dryland training that increases the risk of injury. However, it can also help to prevent injuries. As coach you need to research and understand the effects of weight training before introducing it into a program. The American Swim Coaches Association has an excellent study course on dryland training.

I believe in weight training for some swimmers; most swimmers will develop more strength and speed as a result of it. On the other hand, many great distance coaches do not believe in any weight training; they want to avoid any additional bulk and other possible negative results from the use of weights. I would suggest that distance swimmers be more cautious in their approach to weight training. For example, women will usually benefit most from low-weight and increased repetitions for muscle toning. Caution women swimmers in the extensive use of high-weight and low repetitions; you should approach their weight training based on their individual needs and abilities.

Age-group swimmers who have not gone through puberty should use gymnastics and any other dryland opportunities that meet the requirements of their physical maturity. I don't use weight training for my age-group swimmers, but if you decide to do so, make your decision based on the best research available on the subject.

When I had a weight training room available in my high school, I used it for my boys' team three times a week for about 45 min each session. Because I do not have a weight training room available as a club coach, I use the other forms of dryland training much more extensively in my program.

Making Practices Effective and Fun

If you can make each practice effective and fun, without any conflict, then you have mastered an art in coaching. The greatest fun for swimmers is to swim fast at the season's end in their championship meet. I remind my swimmers of this fact whenever necessary to keep them focused on their goals. However, it is also true that all work and no play makes for dull swimmers.

Every workout must have a purpose in order to be effective. Whenever practical, explain the training plan before practice; although you can't usually do this every day, you should do it often. My swimmers commit to practice with more enthusiasm when they understand the goals of the training plan.

I have used the following methods in practice to provide my swimmers with some light moments and opportunities to relax, while at the same time keeping them focused on their goals.

Starting Practice

Getting swimmers into the water can be a big hurdle each day. I've tried a lot of things from threats to physical assists. Whatever your methods, you'll find that the things that work best are fun for all.

I like the "backstroke flag goggle lag." Swimmers get one chance at the start of practice to throw their goggles onto the backstroke flags line. If their goggles land and hold on the line, they win a healthy power bar from me. Everyone then gets into the water to retrieve their goggles, and practice starts.

I used another fun gimmick to start practice in our outdoor summer pool, where each swimmer got to throw one kickboard from the starting end down the pool. We determined our male and female division winners according to the distance that the kickboard travelled.

Remember, however, that this gimmick requires close supervision to keep all swimmers behind the throwing line until all tosses are completed; otherwise, it could be a safety risk.

GETTING TOO GOOD

The kickboard throw was very popular on my team for several years, but when the young men on one particular team began to throw the kickboards over the fence beyond the length of our 50-m pool on a regular basis, I had to review the contest. I could marshall the pool area but I couldn't control the people and the automobiles in the parking lot, so it was time to change the game.

Right-On Cards

At times we use Tacoma Swim Club Right-On Cards in training. Whenever you catch a teammate doing something right, you make a mental note of it. After practice, you complete a Right-On Card, stating exactly what that swimmer did correctly. Finally, you date, sign, and give the card to the swimmer.

We have had contests each week where the swimmer who gives and receives the most cards gets a prize. This way swimmers can only win if they are both giving and receiving cards. This helps all our swimmers stay positive.

Special Workouts

Your designing a workout by chance, listing training sets and selecting them randomly, is fun for the swimmers. Dart throwing, rolling dice, and drawing cards are good ways to determine training sets.

I conduct a special Christmas Eve workout in the morning, where swimmers can have fun by chancing their way to a "Scrooge" set or a "little elves at play" set. If the swimmers chance their way to a Scrooge, they get hit with an intensive swimming set, but when their chance comes up little elves at play, they get more playful sets.

My favorite little elves at play sets include surf's up, three on two kickboards, whirlpool, stacking kickboards, and tow your buddy. Explanations of each follow. Winners always receive prizes, such as a power bar, fruit, or even a candy cane.

Surf's Up

Have your swimmers stand on the pool bottom and form two lines along two swimming lanes, extending the lines most of the pool's length. Leave one lane open without lines, for a swimmer.

Then, have the swimmers use their kickboards to create as many waves as possible. Select a swimmer to time trial a 50-yd butterfly through the surf.

Whirlpool

Form your swimmers in a large circle in the shallow end; have them walk and then run in a circle, first clockwise, then counterclockwise. Reversing direction is always a major challenge. After a time, get the circle going as fast as possible in one direction, forming a giant whirlpool. Have your swimmers move into the maximum flow and sprint the length of the pool.

Three on Two Kickboards

Three swimmers overlap on two kickboards and they race other such teams through a process of elimination to determine a champion. The middle swimmer of the three holds each of the two kickboards by one arm. The swimmer on the left holds onto the left kickboard with his or her left arm and reaches over the middle swimmer's arm to hold the right kickboard with his or her right. This position is reversed for the swimmer on the right. All three swimmers are shoulder to shoulder on two kickboards.

Stacking Kickboards

In the deep end of the pool, have a swimmer try with both feet to sink a floating kickboard without falling off. Each time a swimmer is eliminated, add one kickboard for those remaining. Subsequent rounds will have two, three, four, and then five or more kickboards until one swimmer is declared champion. The elimination process occurs with a limited number of swimmers going at the same time.

Tow Your Buddy

One swimmer holds the ankle of the leader and is towed for 25 yd, and then the swimmers reverse for the second 25 yd. Teams race off until a winner is declared.

Special Considerations

When do fun items become necessary for your team? When you aren't having fun and aren't excited in the training sessions, you can be certain that your swimmers need a lift too. Change can provide a lift and put a smile on some faces.

You can incorporate a great number of fun items into almost any workout. Relays are always fun; try them with such crazy strokes as the corkscrew stroke and the butterfly with a flutter kick.

Unexpected change is fun. Try having your swimmers run in the pool for part of their repeats. Have them swim a 30×50 with the first and last 12-1/2 yd running instead of swimming. Not only does this provide variety for your swimmers, it also gets their heart rates up for an intense workout.

You can also try handicap relays, where you stagger your swimmers' starts in order to make them play catch up or hold off depending on their positions.

Single file and sprint was one of my favorites in the long course pool. Athletes would swim in a tight single file, and the last one would sprint to the front of the line. When that swimmer took the lead, he or she would slow the pace again, and the new last swimmer would sprint to the front of the line.

Circuit training—moving from one section of the pool to another to complete a circuit—can be a challenging and entertaining change from the usual routine.

How often you insert fun items into your training will depend on the age of your swimmers and your enthusiasm and creativity. If you use special workouts too often, you can lose your focus, and your swimmers can lose interest.

Some fun sessions are best done after practice if time permits. One of my high school teams played a short game of water volleyball after each practice, organizing into teams by class-level. The backstroke flags served as net, and I was the referee. Although our backstroke flags were tattered and torn, our team bond was stronger for playing water volleyball.

Maintaining Focus and Having Fun

One of the best methods I used as a high school coach to maintain focus and have fun doing it involved keeping a season-long point chart. All members of the Wilson High School swim team were listed on that chart and started the season with about 50 minus points; they had to dig their way out of a hole from the very start of the season.

I gave them minus points for everything I could think of: average grades, no long course summer season, a family member who was formerly on the team, long hair, good looks, shyness, or whatever. It used to be a matter of pride when a swimmer ended up with the most minus points, giving him or her bragging rights and creating a few laughs.

Swimmers could earn plus points by having great training habits or by personal-best kicking, pulling, or swimming sets in practice. Personal-best meet times and attaining qualifying time standards for state, Junior Nationals, and Senior Nationals also earned points. Outside of practice and competition, good grades and attendance in school would get them some plus points.

A certain number of points earned a popcorn ball, a milkshake, or an ice cream sundae. On the other hand, a swimmer who ended up with minus points might end up washing my car or cleaning up in my home.

We had a party at our home about 2 weeks before the championship meet, and I paid off the popcorn balls and other prizes to the swimmers. We also used this party to watch meet films of our previous success in state meets and to talk about the coming championship.

Summary

Preparing for practices takes time and creativity from the coach. The following elements can help you better prepare for your training sessions with your swimmers:

1. Make up a written practice schedule.
2. Your practice schedule depends on available pool time.
3. Assign lanes by stroke and distance.
4. Use circle patterns, alternating them by lanes (refer to Figure 6.1).
5. The necessary competitive meet equipment should be in place for practice.
6. Some swimming aids are necessary for maximum individual success.
7. Plan practice sessions to emphasize particular energy systems.
8. Make practice fun while maintaining the focus on goals.
9. Vary your practice plans according to the stage of the season.
10. Supplement your water training with dryland training.

Part III

Coaching Stroke Technique

Chapter 7

Basic Principles in Teaching Strokes

In teaching swimming skills, certain mechanical principles hold true for all four competitive strokes. To swim faster, a swimmer must be able to

- increase propulsion,
- increase tempo, and/or
- decrease resistance.

Most of the time your teaching of strokes will concentrate on increasing propulsion and decreasing resistance. Increasing tempo is an objective in just a few drills, because tempo is usually improved more from the training itself. It is more important for your swimmers first to learn to swim the strokes correctly before building stroke tempo.

Increasing Propulsion

Teach each of your swimmers to attain the maximum distance per stroke from each arm cycle. Holding water effectively and then moving the body past the stroking arms are the keys to increasing propulsion in your learners.

In the 1970s, Dr. Jim Counsilman and others developed the lift theory of propulsion and suggested the value of a sculling motion in all four strokes. This propulsion theory was quite different from the commonly used pull and then push method of armstroking.

However, in the early 1960s, some of us were using what I called the "new water concept"—teaching strokes based on attaining new water on the hand and arms throughout the stroking range. I helped swimmers visualize the sculling process by telling them that the swimmer who took the first armstroke in morning training was holding onto water that had been rooted in one spot since the evening before. That new water provided substantial resistance because it was not yet in motion; however, once it began to move along with the direction of the hand, much of its resistance to hand and arm was gone.

Our swimmers had to move off that one "piece" of water once it got into motion and engage a new piece for better resistance and subsequently more propulsion. With this method I taught swimmers to scull and to move their armstrokes in lateral movements, and I still use it today to help swimmers visualize the concept of sculling their way through water. Diagonal sweeps is another descriptive term for sculling (see Figure 7.1).

In his book, *Swimming Even Faster*, Dr. Ernie Maglischo has established four basic armsweeps used by competitive swimmers—out, down, in, and up.

Decreasing Resistance

Resistance is the amount of water that your swimmer's body displaces while attempting

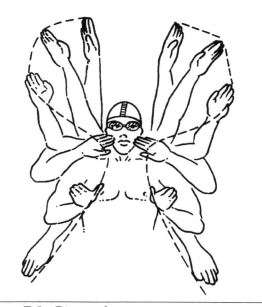

Figure 7.1 Diagonal sweeps.

to move through it. Basically, the more streamlined body will displace less water than its counterpart. Torpedoes can't be shaped like cannon balls and be as effective.

It isn't an accident that fast swimmers in international competition are more often built like race horses than plow horses. Very successful swimmers usually have tapered, streamlined bodies. Though height may not be critical, the best swimmers are tapered from the shoulders to the feet.

You may not be able to change your swimmers' basic body type, but you can help them develop a more tapered body. Swimming requires long periods of stroking with both arms, and that alone helps to fill out the upper body and shoulders. Supplementary dryland training will also help in this regard. For the lower body, kicking drills will slim and firm the hips and thighs. Add good nutritional guidelines to your swimmers' daily energy intake and they will develop a more tapered body.

When you consider how a swimmer moves through water, you can easily see the advantages of a tapered body type. A streamlined body cuts a hole through the water at the head and shoulders. allowing the rest of the body to move through that hole without creating new areas of water resistance at the stomach, hips, or thighs.

Also, water eddies cling to your swimmers' bodies as they move through the water, creating additional resistance. However, if your swimmers are streamlined, they can keep their hips and legs within these eddies both vertically and laterally and avoid creating additional eddies and more resistance.

These principles of propulsion and resistance mentioned here guide all matters of technique and all methods of teaching those techniques. In the next four chapters, I will cover the necessary drills for teaching proper swim technique.

Emphasize Teaching

Take the time necessary to teach, especially early in the season and in those beginning years of each swimmer's career. Each year at Wilson High School, I devoted 30 to 45 min daily to teaching swim skills. This was usually done cross-pool in our diving section. I still do the same thing in my club coaching.

Be persistent and relentless in your teaching. Expect the best and don't let up on your swimmers. Teach, teach, teach!

Teaching Guidelines

I learned a lot about teaching and coaching swimming from a book that wasn't even a swimming book, *Putting the One Minute Manager to Work*, by Kenneth Blanchard and Robert Lorber. The basic principles of this book are as follows:

1. ***Tell the person exactly what he or she did right.*** I believe in strengthening positive mental pictures, so tell your swimmers what they are doing right, not what they are doing wrong. The negative mental picture created when swimmers see what they are doing wrong is not the best opportunity for positive change. On the other hand, if you praise swimmers when they do something positive, they feel good about themselves and what they are doing right. This is a valuable learning tool to use for your swimmers.

2. ***Keep it short and simple.*** This is called the KISS method. Swimmers can only focus on one or very few stroke tips at any given time, so keep your instructions short and simple for the best results. "Elbows up!" "Lengthen your reach!" "Finish your stroke!" All of these statements are concise and serve as positive examples of the KISS method.

Keep coming back to basics when teaching swim skills. Keep your program simple and easy to understand. The best swimmers do it naturally, almost without effort. All strokes flow best when we keep coming back to basics.

BREAKING OUT OF A PLATEAU

When swimmers struggle in competition, back off from focusing on their time measurements. Put your stop watch in your pocket and go back to some basic drills. Let your swimmers focus on the basics of good stroke technique by maximizing their distance per stroke.

This is what I did at state and national championship meets, even at the Olympic Games. Kaye Hall trained on a few basic technique drills for about 6 days before winning her Olympic gold medal and world record. Many Wilson High School swimmers scored at our state championship meet by doing the same type of technique training leading into their competition.

3. ***Never reprimand learners, because reprimands don't teach skills.*** You must be persistent in your teaching but patient with those willing to learn. Swimmers who are trying to acquire advanced skills must do so by learning, so treat them accordingly.

4. ***Watch your swimmers perform.*** Teach a skill and let your swimmers know you care by keeping an eye on them. Watching your swimmers makes them more aware of their need to perfect their skills.

5. ***Praise their progress or redirect their efforts to the task at hand.*** If they aren't ready to proceed, then have them go through the process again.

The following sequence should be repeated until your swimmers develop their skills adequately enough to progress to the next level:

1. Explain the swimming skill to be learned, then have a competent swimmer demonstrate that skill.
2. Have your swimmers attempt the skill through practice.
3. Observe their performance and then either praise their progress or start all over again with the same teaching sequence.

The way in which *Putting the One Minute Manager to Work* provided a logical sequence to my teaching is just one example of how you can use articles and books directed toward other professions to help you in your coaching.

Stroke Coaching

A short time before Howard Firby (the Canadian National and Olympic coach) died, I attended a clinic in Canada where I heard him make a presentation of suggestions for coaching strokes. I am including many of his suggestions in this chapter before going into the specifics for each stroke in the next four.

1. Begin with standard techniques. You can tailor the stroke to each individual's particular ability later.
2. Get the swimmer's timing and general movement correct before concerning yourself with exact or complex actions.
3. Develop the swimmer's skill first and the speed later.
4. Speak to every swimmer every session.
5. Address each swimmer by name.
6. Use common words and avoid academic expressions.
7. Sequence your details, permitting the learner to concentrate on one movement at a time.
8. Be concise and use word pictures, like, "Place your arms out front like a swordfish's sword."
9. Be specific. For example, use your own hand to illustrate a particular movement.
10. Start with something your swimmers already know and build from there.
11. Compliment and then correct.
12. Ask for feedback; have the swimmer teach it back to you.
13. Pick your demonstrators with care. The swimmer demonstrating can be just a notch above the learning group and still be very effective.
14. Be tolerant and patient. If the learner hasn't learned, the teacher hasn't taught.
15. Reward improvement.
16. Persist. Some swimmers need more reminding than others.
17. Avoid being "picky." Don't be forever interrupting swims to fix minor faults; rather, note the problem and treat it at an opportune time.
18. Avoid distractions. Have your swimmers face you with their backs to any possible distractions. If you are sharing a pool with another team, get to the opposite end of that pool.
19. Coach at your swimmers' eye level whenever possible. Crouch or sit at the side of the pool or when necessary, be in the water.
20. Use visual aids. Videotaping is one of the greatest advances in my own coaching career.
21. Use buddy coaching—swimmers coaching each other.

LEARN BY TEACHING

I've used swimmers to teach their teammates certain skills necessary for good technique. The selected swimmer explains the skill and then demonstrates it either through a drill or in the swimming stroke. The swimmer turned teacher always does best when the spotlight is focused on him or her.

My son, Dick Jr., had a two-beat crossover kick when he swam the crawlstroke up to the 10th grade. I had been attempting to change him to a six-beat kick through special kicking drills. During that year, I took him with me to a swimmers' clinic that I was holding in Anchorage, Alaska. I used him as my demonstrator for the drills and the swimming strokes. We went to three different pools, and I had him demonstrate the six-beat kick all through a long day. By the time we returned to Tacoma, he had eliminated his two-beat crossover kick.

I believed Dick Jr. needed a six-beat crawlstroke kick to be successful in short course high school swimming. Two years later, he broke two national high school records as a result of his teaching the skill to others.

22. Make major changes early in the season for national level swimmers and constantly with lower levels.
23. Use stroke drills and progressions.

Summary

1. Teaching technique centers around increasing propulsion and decreasing resistance.
2. Sculling is the application of the "new water" concept.
3. A streamlined and tapered body is best for swimming fast.
4. Take time to teach.
5. Tell your swimmers what they are doing right.
6. Keep it short and simple.
7. Never reprimand a learner.
8. Observe your swimmers' performance.
9. Praise your swimmers' progress or redirect them to the goal at hand.

Chapter 8

Teaching the Crawlstroke

The first task in teaching all of the competitive strokes is to maximize the distance per stroke. Speed and stroke tempo can come later. Counting the strokes taken to reach a given point or cross-pool or one pool length are good indicators of the distance covered by each armstroke. Marking the hand entry and the hand exit points by spotting cones on the pool deck will help swimmers become aware of their distance per stroke. Moving the body past the arm is the desired result of each armstroke. The hand must exit in front of the point of the hand entry, and spotting cones on the deck will indicate if this is being done.

The two most common kicking patterns in the crawl are the six-beat and the two-beat pattern per arm cycle. Some people are more comfortable using a broken tempo kick that isn't a six- or a two-beat kick. Kicking drills will be the same regardless of the number of kicks actually used in each complete arm cycle.

Regardless of the kicking rhythm, the shoulders, hips, and legs must roll throughout the stroke. Body rotation provides additional power and facilitates streamlining.

Stroke Mechanics

There are two major considerations in the area of mechanics: One is the actual technique that is best for each individual swimmer, and the second is the best sequence for teaching the skills necessary for a good crawlstroke.

Technical Aspects

When teaching the crawlstroke, focus your instruction on four main areas: the armstroke, body rotation and streamlining, the kick, and breathing properly.

The Armstroke

The crawlstroke is made up of five phases. It begins with the entry and catch, then a downsweep, followed by the insweep, moving to the upsweep or propulsive finish, and finally into the release and recovery phase. Keeping the elbows high is the most necessary component for successfully mastering these phases.

A high elbow position during the entry phase will help place the arm into the water cleanly with less resistance and will ensure an effective sculling position to start the underwater armstroke. Entry into the water should be made through the same hole with the fingertips entering first, then the wrist, and then the elbow. The hand should enter the water at a point between the eye and the tip of the shoulder on the side of the stroking arm (see Figure 8.1).

Figure 8.1 Hand entry for the crawl.

Push the elbow forward on entry as the hand moves into the catch and begins the downsweep. Pushing the elbow forward will help to hold it

higher than the hand and to maximize the distance per stroke. Don't permit a drop of the elbow at this point in the stroke. Teaching swimmers to just stretch at this point will too often result in a dropped elbow, whereas instructing them to push their elbows forward will more often achieve the desired reach with more control of the high elbow.

The catch position permits swimmers to feel and engage water firmly on the hand at the start of the sculling armsweeps. The palm should be pitched outward with the little finger slightly higher than the thumb. This hand position also helps keep the elbow up (see Figure 8.2). As the arm sweeps downward, it will move slightly outside the shoulder (see Figure 8.3).

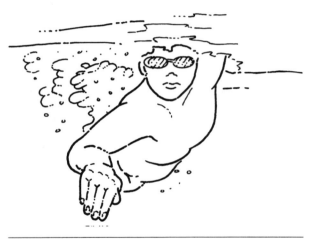

Figure 8.2 The catch position showing a good body roll. The hand presses slightly outward as the elbow starts to bend.

Figure 8.3 Proper positioning for the armsweep—down and out.

The insweep or sculling-in movement is the third phase of the armstroke. Keeping the elbows up during the underwater strokes is a must. There should be no exceptions to this principle, because it is necessary to establish an "anchored" arm position from which the swimmer can effectively push the body past the arm (see Figure 8.4).

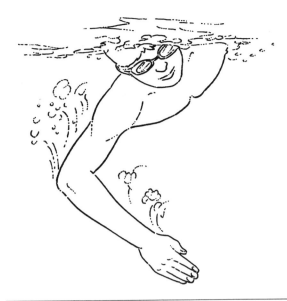

Figure 8.5 The insweep phase of the crawlstroke.

Figure 8.4 The anchored arm position.

The palm is gradually pitched to make the thumb higher than the little finger as it moves to the inward scull. This insweep should come into a position close to or slightly past the midline of the body. Proper execution of this movement will facilitate body rotation, which is discussed later. The arm bends to its greatest angle during this insweep (see Figure 8.5).

The upsweep or final scull in the armstroke is the most propulsive sweep, and when properly done, is known as having a good back half or finish in the armstroke. Rotate the palm of the hand outward again with the little finger higher than the thumb. Push water off the fingertips as the hand position changes on the water. For the only time in the underwater armstroke, the elbow and wrist should lead the hand slightly in order to permit it to push water off the finger-

tips. On the finish of the armstroke, this is a bent wrist position (see Figure 8.6).

The arm accelerates in the back half of the armstroke. As the hand comes close to the thigh on the finish of the stroke, it flips out or "karate chops" to the side to get into the recovery with a minimum of water resistance. When a good release is made, this will get the swimmer into the recovery quickly and smoothly, but if the swimmer continues to push water back, he or she will lose the momentum needed for a good recovery.

An elbows-up position in the recovery would have the elbow higher than the hand (see Figure 8.7). The arm is relaxed and bent at the elbow with the hand under or slightly outside of the elbow. Teach the high elbow recovery in the crawl armstroke. There is an occasional exception to this rule: If the swimmer has good tempo and power, in spite of his or her hand being higher than the elbow in the recovery phase, then don't correct it.

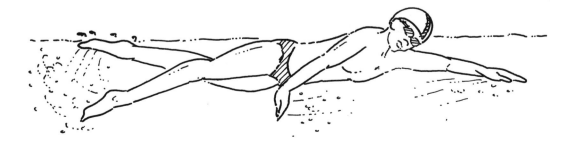

Figure 8.6 A bent wrist is most effective at the finish.

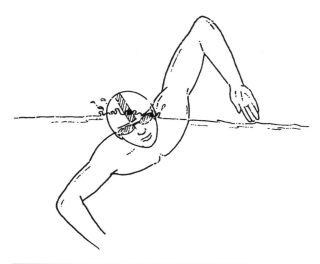

Figure 8.7 The elbow should be higher than the hand in the recovery phase.

Body Rotation and Streamlining

When I was a young competitive swimmer, I was taught to swim as flat on the water as possible. However, after I started coaching, it became obvious to me that this was not the most efficient way to swim. By rotating the body and swimming more on the side, the swimmer's body is streamlined, positioned so it creates less resistance and moves faster through the water.

 **ROTATION AND SPEED**

One of the most memorable demonstrations I have ever witnessed occurred at a clinic about 30 years ago, when Coach Howard Firby stretched out a long piece of surgical tubing that was anchored at one corner of the pool and gave it to a swimmer at the other end. The swimmer, holding onto the end of the tubing, was pulled to the other end of the pool.

Coach Firby performed this demonstration twice—first with the swimmer holding the tubing with both hands extended overhead. The swimmer was timed and observed moving in a near flat position. In the second demonstration, the swimmer held the end of the tubing with only one hand, and as a result naturally turned onto one side. In this position, the swimmer moved considerably faster across the pool and created a much smaller wave in front.

"Tow your buddy," the game you learned in chapter 6, illustrates the principle behind body rotation and streamlining. When the towed swimmer holds onto the other's leg with both hands, he or she stays flat and creates more water resistance. On the other hand, when the swimmer holds onto the leg with *one* hand, he or she rolls to the side and lessens the water resistance. I've

never had any swimmers who have won a tow your buddy race by holding onto the lead swimmer's leg with two hands.

When teaching body rotation and streamlining, have your crawl swimmers picture themselves as though they were skewered on a broom handle. The broom handle is screwed through the top of their head down to their hips. The body moves on that broom handle from side to side, continuously through each arm cycle, without ever breaking or bending that handle. The goal is to keep the body in one straight line throughout the skewered swimmer's side to side movement.

The Kick

The kick in the crawlstroke is not just up and down but is also sideward as it follows a rotating body. The body rotation must be in a straight line, and the legs and feet must also kick within this same line, remaining within the boundaries of the eddies created by the upper half of the body.

The depth and width of the kick have limits. Teach a streamlined, continuous kick from the hips with flexible knees. Use drills like the lateral streamlined kicking and one arm stroking, because they utilize a rotating body position.

Proper Breathing

Breathing drills must be included in your teaching of the crawl. Breathing every one, two, and three strokes are all necessary steps in teaching crawl breathing, but not in that order. Breathing every two strokes on one favorite breathing side is natural and probably the most used method by swimmers. However, swimmers need to practice breathing every three strokes in many of their technique drills, because this forces them to breathe on both sides with a balanced stroke.

Balanced body rotation comes by breathing every three strokes. One side breathing can only result in an uneven body rotation. Breathing every stroke is a drill used less often, but I like it to develop faster body rotation. When swimmers breathe every stroke, they develop more hip rotation, or what's known as a hip "pop," that increases their hand speed in the stroke's power phase and speeds them into the recovery.

Breathing while skewered and rotating on a broom handle must result in straight line swimming. Teach your swimmers to breathe in the trough created by the head as it turns to the side to breathe. As the swimmer's chin follows the shoulder in the body rotation, the head is turned on its side with the ear in the water; the swimmer's eyes should focus on the water surface just a few inches ahead of the mouth as it opens to breathe. This breathing position will keep the majority of your swimmers in a straight line on the skewer during all phases of their body rotation (see Figure 8.8).

Figure 8.8 For a good breathing position, the eyes should be focused on the water surface just in front of the mouth, and the ear on the water side of the face should be in the water.

Teach your swimmers to breathe without holding their breath. They should exhale slowly at first and time their exhalation so that they can finish with a burst of air as their mouth clears the water surface.

Sequence of Teaching Crawl

I would teach a basic armstroking skill first to give your swimmers some confidence in their ability to move through the water effectively. In those first drills, I would also establish a basic armstroke technique. In waist-deep water, use a walking drill called the hand, wrist, elbow drill (see p. 74).

The torpedo streamlined position must be taught as one of the first drills (see p. 75), followed by the kicking and breathing skills. Next, teach the armstroking drills of sculling and maximizing distance per stroke. With each of these skills effectively in place,

you can begin to concern yourself with timed speed drills.

Crawlstroke Starts, Turns, and Finishes

Once you've taught and had your swimmers practice their starts, turns, and finishes, you must incorporate those drills into your practice sessions that permit all three skills to be improved through perfect practice. Mental training is also necessary. Have swimmers visualize doing perfect starts, turns, and race finishes. Develop relaxation drills, such as controlled deep breathing or lying down and listening to some easy music, to put your swimmers into a state conducive to mental visualization.

Front Starts

Prior to your swimmers' start, encourage them to maintain good circulation, especially in their hands and feet. The use of dry footwear, gloves, and warm-ups will help them avoid becoming cold and losing the feel for the water. Have them use a dry towel to wipe the starting block and their feet and hands. While swimmers are seated or waiting, have them avoid crossing their legs or arms. Such reminders to your swimmers will promote adequate circulation. Teach them to relax before the starting signal, and they will have a quick reaction.

When teaching your swimmers the "take your mark" position, tell them to concentrate on staying on the balls of their feet and not letting their heels touch the block. They should focus on exploding off the blocks at the starting signal.

Teach the following for your swimmers' stance on the blocks:

1. Toes slightly in
2. Heels slightly out
3. Knees slightly bent
4. Head down or looking down the pool
5. Upper body as high as possible
6. Elbows straight or nearly so
7. Fingers and thumb inside or outside of the feet and gripping the forward edge of the block
8. Total concentration on the starting signal (see Figure 8.9)

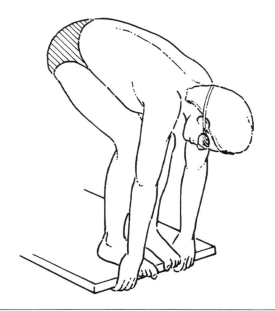

Figure 8.9 The starting stance for the crawl.

At the starting signal, the head leads, the hands follow, and the body finishes the action. Emphasize each of the following:

1. Flex the arms first and pull toward the water.
2. Get out, not up, straight from the blocks. Thrust the arms to a 90° angle with the head just above the shoulders. Get out as far as possible.
3. Through the legs, drive off the blocks with the entire body.
4. Drop the head between the shoulders and the upper arms just before water entry.

5. Hyperextend to a full torpedo position on entry.
6. Use a hand-on-hand entry through a small hole, kicking out or whipping out, to get the legs through that hole.
7. Point your toes on entry and glide only long enough to take full advantage of the dive momentum (see Figure 8.10).

Many swimmers prefer the track start. Swimmers begin with both feet forward, step back with one leg, and keep the heel up on the back leg. The back leg should be positioned well back on the blocks. Swimmers should grip tight, lean back, drive off the back leg first, and then throw themselves into a normal starting position off the front leg at the starting signal. Relay starts should utilize a form of rolling start. Swimmers shouldn't use grab starts on relays.

Teaching tips for the crawl start would include:

1. Swimmers hold the velocity as long as possible by kicking hard and using shallow and very quick flutterkicks as soon as they enter the water.
2. Accelerate the first arm pull all the way through the finish. The swimmer's head should still be under the surface water tension until near the finish of the first armstroke.
3. Finish the pull, lift the head, and break out or "surf" through the surface.
4. Swimmers should ride the water high as they go into the first surface armstroke. Have them stretch the non-

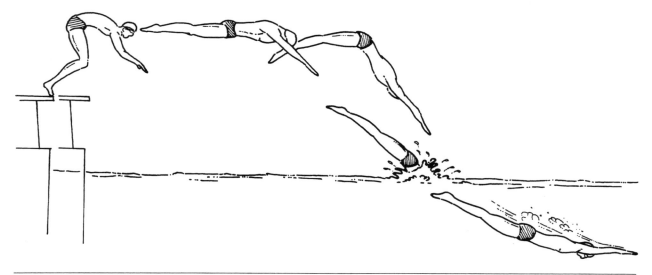

Figure 8.10 The start through entry positions for the crawl.

pulling arm out front during the first surface stroke to streamline as much as possible.

Turns

The key to great turns is to teach, expect, and demand them in practice. Emphasize the following steps in teaching the crawl turn:

1. Swimmers must build speed on the approach to every wall, because the momentum they have going into the wall will determine how fast they get off from it; the faster they can come into a wall, the faster they will come off it.
2. Get the nose to the knees and the heels to the hips on the turn. Teach a compact tuck position for your swimmers' turns.
3. Swimmers should pull out with the lower arm first and shouldn't breathe on this first armstroke.
4. Swimmers must kick off the wall with very fast, shallow kicks before breaking into their normal kicking range.
5. Streamline into the full torpedo position off each wall underwater and under the surface tension (see Figure 8.11).

Finishes

Your swimmers should finish with an arm fully stretched and their body rolled to one side; this position will give them added inches to the length of their arm at the finish. Your swimmers must keep their ear on their shoulder at the finish so that their head remains in the water through the completion of the wall touch. Emphasize that they keep the flutterkick going—so as to drive themselves into the wall—until they complete the wall touch.

The value of an efficient race finish can't be overemphasized. I'm especially proud of my swimmers when they win the close ones. Close races are won by the swimmers who have practiced great finishes. Frequently in my practice sessions, I include a few minutes at the end of a workout for finish drills.

⚬⚬ **WINNING CLOSE RACES**

Several years ago, I started doing finish drills on a frequent basis throughout the season. The first season we won two very close races

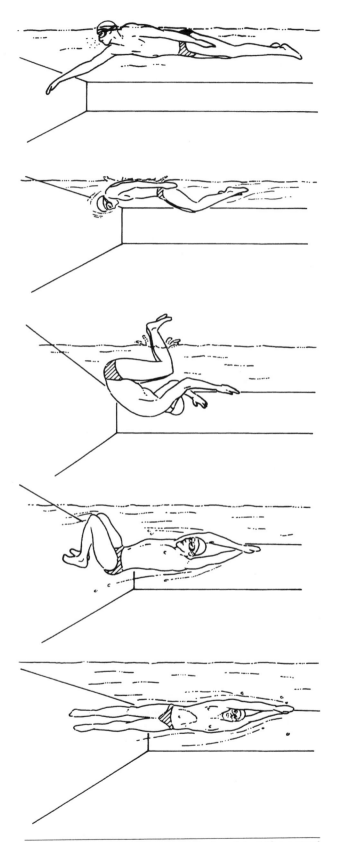

Figure 8.11 The five steps in teaching the crawl turn.

because of that special training emphasis on finishes. In a major meet in Las Vegas, one of our high school girls held on to win an 800-yd free relay for our Tacoma Swim Club against some good college swimmers. Also, one of our high school boys at the high school state championship meet in the 100-yd free out-touched a rival who appeared to be slightly ahead.

Special Tips for Teaching the Crawlstroke

Drills are the most effective method of teaching stroke skills, so make sure your swimmers do drills correctly. You can isolate stroking technique points through drills and combine these points into the complete stroking pattern.

Be a teacher when using stroke drills. Drills need to be explained, demonstrated, and practiced until your swimmers perform them correctly—this is the key to your swimmers learning effectively. Correct drills, utilizing the best in technique, make perfect practice possible. Don't tolerate drills being done incorrectly. Be exact and expect the best from your swimmers.

Feel of the Water

Teach your swimmers to use their fists only in some drills or while swimming crawl. Then, have them gradually open the hand to better feel the water. Closing the fists removes the sensation of water on the hand; however, when your swimmers reopen their hands, they, as a result of the previous absence of sensation, will have a better perception of the hand on water. Additional methods of creating water awareness include having your athletes swim with their fingers making the "A-OK" sign or swimming only with the index or "pinky" finger extended to attain better feel of the water.

Similarly, use hand paddles in the same way to attain a better feel. For the best results, you should use both versions of holed paddles, Han's Paddles and Grippers (see chapter 6).

Fins

Use fins in at least some of your kicking and swimming drills to increase your swimmers' speed and confidence in both areas. Fins also help to streamline the legs while kicking. Try all sizes and shapes of fins to determine what's best for your swimmers. I prefer a soft-shoe type of fin that is comfortable on my swimmers' feet. For the best results, I cut a few inches off the end of these flippers to allow the swimmer to kick at swimming speed. With these shorter fins, your swimmers can kick faster and in the correct range.

Distance and Endurance Considerations

Your teaching of the basic crawl should be the same for all of your swimmers; only when they specialize in a particular sprint or distance event will there be some differences that you need to recognize.

Swimmers at 200 m and longer distances in crawl will need to breathe every stroke cycle in most instances. Swimmers with a two-beat or broken tempo kick are stroking faster and can breathe every three strokes or 1-1/2 cycles. In these longer events, sustained speed is the goal, and regular breathing makes this a better possibility; teach these swimmers to breathe every cycle or as I have indicated here.

Distance swimmers, with the water level nearer their hairlines, will have a lower head position than sprinters. The sweeping or sculling action of your distance crawl swimmers might be more pronounced than that of your sprinters. This occurs with some swimmers in overdistance training.

Drills for the Crawl

I will outline a number of drills that I believe are necessary in teaching new skills or in perfecting learned ones. Some of these drills I rarely use or use only with certain swimmers who may need that special drill. Once your swimmers learn these drills, they can keep coming back to basics by incorporating them into their practice sessions and their warm-ups at competition. I will list the major drills in a sequence that I would highly recommend for teaching crawl swimming, but they would not have to be introduced in this exact order.

Hand, Wrist, Elbow

Teach the standing hand, wrist, elbow drill first in this series. Have your swimmers stand in waist-deep water and simulate the crawl armstroke. Isolate or freeze the entry point, hand pitch, high elbow arm recovery, the pushing of the elbow forward on entry, and the sweeps or sculling sections of the armstroke.

Direct the entry

1. fingertips and hand first,
2. then wrist,
3. and then elbow.

Talk to your swimmers. Call out hand, wrist, elbow as the arm goes through this sequence on entry. Have your swimmers also call out this sequence as they go through the hand, wrist, elbow entry (see Figure 8.12).

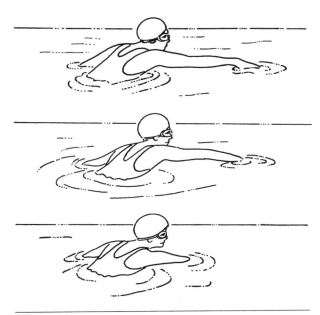

Figure 8.12

Once you've taught your swimmers the standing drill, have them begin walking through this same drill in waist-deep water. Emphasize that they walk past the hand on each stroke so that they can feel the distance covered in each armstroke. As they walk, the swimmers will be able to see the point of hand entry and see themselves get past that point at the hand exit position.

Move from the walking drill to swimming short distances with emphasis on the hand, wrist, elbow drill. Have your swimmers mentally repeat these words—hand, wrist, elbow—while swimming, just as they verbally called them out in the standing and walking drills. I like to move from a couple of strokes standing, to walking a few strokes, and then to swimming the drill for a short distance.

Torpedo

Torpedo is the full-body streamlined position with both arms extended overhead. One hand is on top of the other hand with the thumb of the top hand gripped around the little finger side of the lower hand. Elbows are pulled in tight and the arms are extended. The stomach and buttocks are pulled in tight, and the legs are together and extended fully all the way through the toes. The upper arms are squeezed in just behind the swimmer's ears. This presents a nearly straight line all the way from the top of the swimmer's hands to his or her feet.

Have your swimmers lie on their backs on the pool deck, and make them practice the torpedo position before going into the water. You can adjust some of their faults easily on the deck, emphasizing necessary points by applying some manual pressure where necessary. Practice in the water from push-offs that are just under the water and its surface tension.

Add a flutterkick to the drill when your swimmers have learned to hold a perfect torpedo position. Teach this for short distances underwater that are comfortable and safe for the level of your swimmers.

Streamlined Lateral Kicking

This kicking drill is done in a lateral position. Assume the maximum rotation position of the crawlstroke by extending one arm forward and keeping the other arm at the opposite side of the body. Teach this lateral stretch position precisely, with the extended arm on the lower side of the body and in a spear position as straight as possible with the little finger and the elbow tipped up slightly. The other arm on the higher side is extended back alongside the leg.

Holding the spear position, with the little finger and elbow tipped up, is critical for this lateral drill to be effective. Do not permit a dropped elbow at any time. Practice this drill first on one side and then the other for a given distance, either one length or cross-pool (see Figure 8.13).

Once this streamlined position has been learned correctly, you can teach swimmers

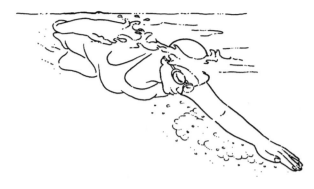

Figure 8.13

to do 12/12, 8/8, and 6/6 combination drills. In the 12/12 kicking drill, the swimmer kicks 12 times on one side and then rotates and does another 12 kicks on the other side. Holding the speared arm position correctly throughout the 12 kicks and through the rotation on the other side is critical. A 10/10 would include 10 kicks, a rotation, then 10 more; an 8/8 and 6/6 would include the listed number of kicks, a rotation, then the remaining kicks.

I like combining this kicking drill so that my swimmers start with a 12/12, then go into a 10/10, then an 8/8, and finally a 6/6. Each repeat of this drill would start and finish the same way. One example might be 10 x 75 yd: Wherever our swimmers are in their kick count cycle, when they get to 6/6, they would hold that kick until that 75 was completed, and then they would start anew in the next 75.

Breathing

Breathing drills can start at anytime and can be combined into some of the drills that I have already listed. Bobbing drills, which teach rhythmic breathing, start early for any new swimmer. These can be done in 4 or 5 ft of water while standing on the bottom of the pool or even in deep water while holding onto the side of the pool or staying away from the wall. Use bobbing to teach your swimmers the timing of inhaling and exhaling.

You can add breathing to the hand, wrist, elbow drill once it is learned. The standing drill helps swimmers learn to time their breathing to their armstroke and to develop the correct in-line position of the head when breathing. Breathing is next added to the hand, wrist, elbow walking drills and then the swimming drills.

You can emphasize the proper head position in breathing with the streamlined kicking drills, and then you can add the breathing timing in the one-arm swim drills.

One-Arm Swims With One Arm Extended

This drill follows the streamlined lateral kicking drills. Emphasize the forward extended position of the speared arm. Your swimmers must keep their little finger and elbow tipped up at all times in this drill. Have your swimmers do the crawlstroke with only the one arm that had been at their side during the streamlined lateral kicking drill. They should continue to extend and spear their forward arm as they swim the crawl with one arm (see Figure 8.14).

Figure 8.14

This is a great streamlining and maximum distance per stroke drill. Changing the stroking arm every length or every specified number of strokes helps to develop an even stroke through the body rotation cycle and to facilitate the swimmers' ability to breathe to both sides. Breathing takes place on the side of the stroking arm.

Sculling

Teaching swimmers to scull and use practice drills in sculling is one of the most neglected areas in coaching. I designed and manufactured a special hand paddle that I believe is the best aid in teaching and improving sculling skills. The Gripper (listed under swim aids in chapter 6) has a grooved paddle on its water side that assists greatly in developing and accelerating sculling feel by emulating the feel of the hand itself on the water.

The first sculling position that I teach is the front extended breaststroke position for sculling. My swimmers approximately 12 years and older use the Gripper for this sculling drill. Teach your swimmers to keep their hands high on the water, very close to the surface. Have them scull out by pitching their hands outward or with the little finger higher than the thumb, and scull in by pitching their hands inward or with the thumb higher than the little finger. They should keep the scull continuous with pressure on the forearms. This is my main sculling drill, and I believe it should be used daily.

Teach the other sculling positions for crawl, such as the midpull position under the shoulders, also known as the windshield wiper position and the finish position (see Figure 8.15). I like to add the synchronized-swimming sculling skill with the swimmers on their backs, moving in a reverse direction, with their arms either overhead or at their sides. These last two skills are used only to increase the sculling feel for swimmers, and they are not our main sculling skills.

Figure 8.15

Maximum Distance Per Stroke

After you teach the previous skill drills, you can either move on to other drills or directly into those that maximize distance per stroke. Counting the number of strokes for one pool length or pool width is an easy and effective method to use. A more advanced drill is the minimum-number drill and it appears on page 78.

Additional Drills

There are many additional drills you can use in your teaching to improve the crawlstroke, a number of which I'll list shortly. Consider the drills that I have already outlined for crawl as major ones that I recommend highly for your consideration.

Stretch-Up Swims

Because of their similarity, stretch-up swims should follow one-arm swims with the arm extended forward. The former drill is the same as the latter, except the swimmer switches to the other arm after each stroke. Both drills stress the main technique points. Stretch-up swims refer to the swimmer having one arm stretch up to the other before stroking with that other arm. It is a complete overlapping stroke. Emphasize pushing the elbow forward on entry to control its position better. Although stretch-up swims are good for maximum distance per stroke, they can lead to a dropped elbow position in your swimmers, so use them sparingly with an eye on quality control.

Chicken Wing

Chicken wing drills are for high elbow recovery. Full chicken wing involves stroking with the arms while the thumbs are hooking the armpits (see Figure 8.16). In the

Figure 8.16

one-quarter chicken wing, the swimmer strokes the arms with the fingers no longer hooking the armpits but just off of that position. In the one-half chicken wing, the swimmer strokes the arms with the fingers hanging down directly under the elbows. Because you use this drill only to remind swimmers to get their elbows up, have them swim short distances (e.g., 25 yds).

One-Arm Swims With the Nonstroking Arm at the Side

This is one-arm swimming with the non-stroking arm at the side (see Figure 8.17). You should teach your swimmers to breathe on the opposite side of their stroking arm and to time their head turn for breathing to the entry of the stroking arm. This drill also requires swimmers to focus more on maintaining the skewered and streamlined swimming position. Once your swimmers learn the drill, have them alternate their breathing side, which will help balance their body rotation.

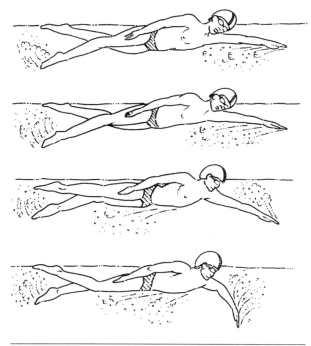

Figure 8.17

Thumb Drag

Use the thumb drag for teaching a high elbow on the arm recovery. Your swimmers recover their arm by dragging the thumb along the body through the armpit. Variations of this drill would be to have your swimmers' "fingers do the walking" on the water through their recovery. A similar drill is the "zipper" recovery whereby your swimmers zipper the hand to the body during the recovery.

Heads Up Crawl

Both a power and a high elbow drill, the heads up crawl shortens the stroke and consequently doesn't aid in maximizing distance per stroke. However, because it has power and elbow position value, it is a good drill for your sprint swimmers.

Swim the Rope

Stretch a rope the length of your pool and anchor it at both ends, preferably a few inches underwater. Have your swimmers swim the rope by straddling it, gripping it with each hand, and pulling themselves past the gripping hand. This activity teaches maximum distance per stroke and gives your swimmers the feeling of moving the body with the arm. Count the number of strokes your athletes need to swim each length on the rope. Have them return to the other end without swimming on the rope and again count their strokes. They should attempt to maintain the same number of strokes.

Minimum-Number Swims

In this drill, your athletes should swim a given distance, say, for example 50 yd, and count the number of strokes that they took and record their time. This will determine their minimum number. Minimum-number swims are designed to equate your swimmers' race-pace split time with their most efficient number of strokes. For example, if your swimmer has a time of 28.5 s in the 50 yd and requires 31 strokes to complete the distance, then he or she would have a total number of 59.5. If the same swimmer completes the 50 yd again with a time of 28.2 s in 32 strokes, then he or she would have a total number of 60.2.

In these two examples the best minimum number is 59.5. You would have your swimmers do repeat 50s with the goal of attaining this total number. In this particular example, the minimum number of 59.5 might indicate the best possible pace for a

200-yd race. However, remember that your swimmers' numbers will change as they train. About once a week, you should retest your swimmers and redefine their goals based upon their new minimum numbers.

Transition Drills

Combining drills to follow a logical progression can be an effective way to teach the crawlstroke. Have your swimmers focus on one drill, then move them to others, until they are doing the complete stroke. The transition from drills to regular swimming will carry their good technique forward.

For example, have your swimmers start with a lateral streamlined kick, then progress to one-arm swims with one arm extended, then to stretch-up swims, and then finally to swimming crawl.

You might also start with a full chicken wing, then move to a quarter chicken wing, then to a half chicken wing, and then finally to swimming crawl.

Another possible progression of drills might include: a dog paddle with the head up, a crawl arm pull with underwater recovery and the head up or down, a tip of the elbow out of the water with head up or down, a half arm lift with head down, a wrist drag, a fingertip drag, and then finally swimming crawl. I list these examples only to give you an idea of the countless combinations that you can use to organize your drills into a logical progression.

Summary

The following hints will help you to teach and coach great crawl:

1. You can permit a variety of kicking rhythms to each armstroke, but teach a continuous kick.
2. Maximize distance per stroke first; speed can come later.
3. Emphasize high elbows.
4. Stress to your swimmers that their entry is hand, then wrist, then elbow.
5. Have your swimmers push their elbow forward on entry.
6. These armsweeps compose sculls: down and out, in, and finish or up.
7. Teach your swimmers to rotate their bodies as if they were on a skewer.
8. Remember that the depth and width of your swimmers' kicks have limits.
9. Have your swimmers focus their eyes on the water surface just in front of their mouth when breathing.
10. Teach a basic armstroke first, then the torpedo position, and then kicking.
11. Prepare your swimmers both mentally and physically for front starts.
12. Your athletes must start by going out and not up.
13. Teach your swimmers to dive through one hole.
14. Expect and demand great turns in practice.
15. Teach your swimmers the correct race finish position.
16. Use drills to teach technique.
17. Demand perfection in your drill practice.
18. Remember that sculling is a major ingredient in successful crawl swimming.
19. Require regular and frequent breathing patterns in your distance swimmers when competing.

Chapter 9

Teaching the Backstroke

The backstroke is similar to the crawlstroke in basic technique, but the number of kicks to each arm cycle does not have the variations seen in the crawl. The six-beat kick is most often preferred and should be taught to your backstrokers.

Additionally, you need to teach the butterfly kick, because swimmers use it in the backstroke while underwater on the start and the turns. Current rules permit up to 15 m of back butterfly kick off each wall prior to surfacing. For many backstroke swimmers, it is faster to do the underwater butterfly kick off each wall than to surface and swim backstroke.

Most swimmers maintain the fast momentum of the push-off in the backstroke's start and turns more efficiently by using the dolphin kick instead of the flutter kick underwater prior to surfacing. All swimmers are different, so you will need to teach and have them practice this skill in order to determine those who will benefit from using the underwater butterfly kick off the walls.

When compared to crawl, the other major difference in backstroke is in the breathing and the relative arm positions. Breathing in the backstroke is not as significant an issue as it is in the crawl, because the face is always out of the water while swimming. The relative arm position in the backstroke—one arm is almost opposite the other—differs greatly from that of the crawl, where there is always a significant overlapping of the arms.

The principles of body roll and of kicking within the width and depth of the body eddies apply in backstroke as they did in crawl. Maximizing the distance per stroke is always a major consideration in all four of the competitive strokes.

The high elbow in the crawl applies to both the recovery and the underwater stroke, but in the backstroke, the underwater stroke needs to be an elbows-down position to best hold water and to attain the maximum distance per stroke. The backstroke arm recovery is quite different from crawl; the swimmer recovers the arm vertically with the hand as its highest part.

Sculling sweeps provide "new" water for the backstroker during the underwater armstroke. Sculling down, up, down again, and finally up again at the finish and into the recovery appears to me to be the best pattern. Some swimmers scull down, up, and then down again and recover from this position. However, I teach the final up scull to finish off the propulsion and to get into the recovery with a faster stroking tempo.

Stroke Mechanics

Consider first the technique that you want to teach to your backstrokers and then the sequence of teaching skills that you will use. I will follow this same procedure for all four competitive strokes.

Technical Aspects

I teach the kick first in backstroke, although you may elect to teach a basic armstroke first to give your swimmers the feeling of moving through the water by armstroking. The walking drills of the crawl don't work well in backstroke. I don't recommend walking drills for teaching backstroke, because walking backward is awkward. I believe that it is much easier to teach the armstroke *after* the backstroke kick is learned. Teaching the skills in this order ensures that swimmers will have a good kick for their backstroke.

Kicking

Teach your swimmers to kick within the body's width and depth and with a loose ankle. Swimmers should kick to the surface with a no-splash kick. As in the crawl, teach a streamlined, continuous kick from the hips with a flexible knee. Use drills that utilize a rotating body position. The skewered body theory of the crawlstroke also applies to the backstroke.

Armstroking

The entry is just short of the 12 o'clock position with each arm. Shoulders and hips rotate or roll on the skewer through the stroke. One arm starts a new stroke just a fraction before the other finishes its stroke (see Figure 9.1).

Figure 9.1   One arm enters just before the other arm finishes.

The entry should be on the little finger side of the hand with the palm facing outward. This will facilitate an effective downsweep, a deep enough catch for the coming upsweep, and a full body rotation.

As in the crawl, the body must rotate on a skewer. The ideal head position should be a stable one. I *have* had backstrokers who have been effective turning their head slightly from side to side, but such a practice risks lateral movement, which can be detrimental to the stroke. On the positive side, turning the head slightly can introduce a roll that facilitates a hip pop and a strong power sweep, especially on the final upsweep. If you have swimmers who can attain a more effective roll in their stroke by slight head turning, analyze them carefully before putting them on drills to eliminate their head movement, especially when it is in line and remains on the skewer.

 OLYMPIAN EXAMPLE

John Naber, a University of Southern California swimmer, had a slight head roll in his backstroke, but he set world records in backstroke events, and he won the gold medals in both backstroke events of the 1976 Montreal Olympic Games.

The depth of the pull and the amount of arm bend in it is an individual consideration, based on the flexibility and strength of each swimmer. Teach the general stroking pattern and then permit swimmers to develop their own most effective method for maximizing their distance per stroke.

The swimmers' hip roll in backstroke initiates the arm recovery. When the hips roll away from the stroking arm as it finishes the underwater armstroke, the shoulder and arm can start the recovery.

At the vertical high point in the recovery, backstrokers should be able to sight down their arm as though it were a rifle barrel. In recovery, the arm should be straight and in a vertical position directly over the shoulder (see Figure 9.2).

The palm of the hand faces in during the first half of the recovery. In the second half, it will rotate so that it faces out. I prefer to consider the second half of the recovery as the entry phase.

Teach a thumb first exit, because it contributes the most propulsion in the final sculling upsweep in the underwater armstroke. Some swimmers exit the water with the back of the hand, but I don't recommend this, because it eliminates or reduces the final upsweep. Although I might tolerate this back of the hand exit in some swimmers, I don't consider it the most desirable method. You should never permit a little finger exit at the finish of the underwater stroke, because it interferes with too many good stroking considerations that I will be emphasizing in this chapter.

Body Positioning

The swimmers' heads should be back just far enough to get on the bow wave. Sitting too much, or tucking the chin too tightly, can keep your swimmers short of that bow wave and create unnecessary resistance by putting their hips too deep in the water.

On the other hand, if your swimmers hold their heads back too far, their hips will be too high and they will lose the effectiveness of their kick. Have your swimmers picture their bodies as shaped a little like a canoe, with the shoulders slightly concave like the canoe's sides. The head should tilt up slightly, similar to the front end of the canoe. This position will create the least resistance to moving through the water in the backstroke (see Figure 9.3).

Figure 9.2 The rifle barrel recovery.

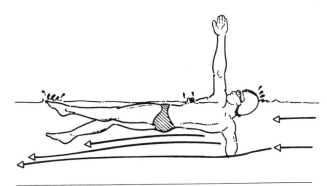

Figure 9.3 The tip of canoe head position.

Sequence of Teaching Backstroke

Teach the kick first and emphasize the torpedo position as I outlined it in chapter 8. Body position comes next or within the kicking drills. Armstroking follows with a major emphasis on sculling drills. Maximize your swimmer's distance per stroke before introducing timed speed drills.

There is no single sequential method that best teaches the backstroke. You have to adjust your methods to fit your levels of swimmers and to fit your strong points as coach. In general, I would normally choose the following sequence:

1. Kicking at the edge of the pool while sitting out of the water
2. Kicking with both arms at the side
3. Torpedo kicking underwater for short distances
4. Lateral streamlined kicking
5. Mirror-arm stroking
6. One-arm swims
7. Full stroke swims

Next, I would begin to work on those drills that I consider necessary to the development of great backstroke: touch down, stop and go, and breakwater drills.

Backstroke Starts, Turns, and Finishes

The same principles for teaching and practicing crawlstroke starts, turns, and finishes hold true in the backstroke. Expect perfect practice and tolerate no exceptions to it, if you want the best in competition.

Back Starts

For the backstroke start, international, U.S. swimming, and collegiate rules require the swimmer to be on the wall with the toes underwater. At the time of writing this book, high school rules permit the stand-up starting position in backstroke. In this particular back start, the swimmer stands in the gutter, crouched over the starting blocks. Either type of back start should be practiced only in deep water, and the stand-up start only in diving-pool-depth water.

The conventional wall start can be broken down into six categories:

1. **Feet placement.** The feet should be placed on the wall at about armpit width. After placing the feet, the toes should turn to the inside to help spread them slightly and help them stick to the wall. The hips should be kept away from the heels. The toes should be kept high, just below the surface and on the same plane. Swimmers should force the toes into the wall and not down the wall.

2. **The grip.** Swimmers should place their thumbs on the upside of the backstroke starting bar.

3. **On the wall and start.** Swimmers must keep the head and back lined up, or curl the head into the blocks slightly. The heels are not quite on the wall. On the command, "Take your mark," the swimmer should pull up as high as is comfortable to the level of gravity (see Figure 9.4). The hips are about 80° to 90° away from the heels.

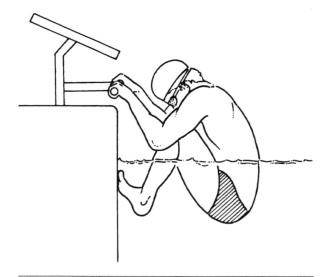

Figure 9.4 The backstroke start on the wall.

4. **Off the wall.** Swimmers should get some snap from the head and use the upper body in the throw. The hands, head, and shoulders should snap back at once. The arms are just ahead of the legs, and the legs must explode off the wall. Swimmers should lift the

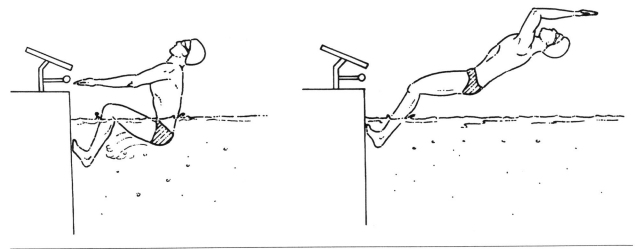

Figure 9.5   The backstroke start off the wall.

core of the body by throwing the arms back in an upward direction as they leave the wall, and then throw the arms down and around. This will bring the hips up over the water and will set up the entry (see Figure 9.5).

5. **Entry.** Swimmers should dive through the entry with the upper body (see Figure 9.6). On entry swimmers must lift the legs and get to the streamlined torpedo position. Have your swimmers break into the kick with small, fast butterfly kicks to get the most momentum off of the dive. Swimmers should use this kick only to the momentum peak or no further than the 15 m of underwater kicking that's permitted by the rules. Then swimmers should switch to the flutter kick for the breakout.

6. **Breakout.** Swimmers should start the second arm pull earlier than in normal backstroke swimming on the

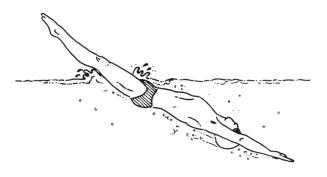

Figure 9.6   Proper entry for the backstroke.

breakout. The arms overlap in this second arm pull, and as a result, pop swimmers up with more momentum into their regular surface strokes. Swimmers must get up on the breakout, get the hips up, and drive with the flutter kick.

If your swimming rules permit the stand-up start, you may want to use it. It is faster for most swimmers, but it requires very deep water for practice and competition. Safety should be your first consideration before making any decision on the use of the stand-up start for backstrokers.

In the stand-up start, swimmers should keep the heels of their hands in contact with the corners of the starting platform, so they have a solid surface to push against. At the starting signal, swimmers must push back with the hands and then continue with the same steps as in the conventional back start.

Turns

Teach your backstrokers the roll turn. Have them gauge their distance from the wall by using the backstroke flags; they should roll over and execute a forward flip turn on the final approach (see Figure 9.7). Make certain that you always have backstroke flags in place and practice legal turns only. Swimmers can leave their back as they begin the final arm recovery and take one stroke as they somersault into the turn on their front. This turn is to be executed in one continuous motion, and no hand touch is required.

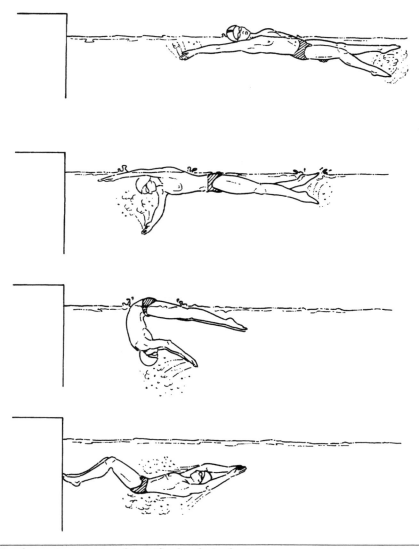

Figure 9.7   The four steps in teaching the backstroke turn.

Teach your swimmers to build their speed as they go into the wall. Backstrokers, in particular, are guilty of slowing down their stroking tempo as they approach the wall. You need to take their stroke rates in their wall approach to remind them to accelerate at these points in the race.

Most backstrokers should do several fast back butterfly kicks off of each wall before going back into their flutter kick on the breakout strokes. The number of butterfly kicks will depend on the individual ability of the swimmer and the rules restricting underwater kicking distances.

Finishes

Teach your backstroke swimmers to finish in a manner similar to the crawl finish, with an arm fully stretched and the body rolled to the side but still legally on the back. Swimmers must keep their head well back through the wall touch and keep kicking to drive them into the wall.

Special Tips for Teaching Backstroke

As in crawl, drills are your most effective teaching method. However, drills must be taught and practiced correctly in order to be effective. Explain, demonstrate, and practice each drill until it is correct. Be persistent and relentless in expecting the best from your swimmers in every drill practice.

Fins

Fins are very important in backstroke swimming development. You can use fins in any of the kicking or swimming drills, and by cutting them shorter, you will enable your backstrokers to kick close to their actual swimming speed. Use a mono-fin—a large single fin with inserts that hold both feet— to teach the back butterfly kick that your swimmers may use off each wall in the start and turns.

Distance and Endurance Considerations

The racing distances in backstroke only extend to 200 yd (meters). This probably does not warrant teaching a different stroking style. Successful 100 and 200 backstrokers will often have only slight differences in their stroke characteristics. For example, a faster stroking tempo for the 100 back may decrease the amount of body roll and may make the swimmer's sweeps less pronounced, but this should not change your method of teaching.

Sustained speed is very important in both the 100 and 200, but more important in the 200. Minimum-number drills are very important to the 200 backstroker.

Drills for the Backstroke

What follows are the drills that I consider necessary for teaching new or improved backstroke skills. Some of these may not be necessary in your particular coaching situation, and the order that these drills are introduced may be different.

You need to use several drills that were outlined in chapter 8. The minimum-number drill is the same in backstroke as it was in crawl. Also, all of the drills used in crawl to develop a swimmer's feel of the water, such as progressing from fists to the full hand, should be used in backstroke as well.

Kicking at the Pool Edge

Have your swimmers sit in the gutter, when the gutter width permits it, and lean back on their elbows on the pool deck. Have them kick gently with a rotating foot action and loose ankles. Your young swimmers can pretend that they are flipping slippers off their feet by rotating each foot as they kick. This kicking drill may not be needed for your more advanced swimmers.

Kicking With Arms at Sides

This is a good drill to establish the swimmers' body position for backstroke. Have swimmers kick with both arms at their sides and with their ears in the water. Your swimmers should focus their eyes on the ceiling at the point from which they are moving. They can tuck the chin slightly to accommodate this eye position. In outdoor pools, the only way to control this eye position is by the chin tuck.

Look at the depth of your swimmers' hips and their kick. Watch how the head rides on the bow wave from an elevated position. If the head isn't back on the bow wave, or if the hips and kick are too deep, then adjust the head position by having swimmers look more directly overhead and reduce their chin tuck. If the hips are too high, or the head is back too far, have them adjust by tucking the chin more and looking back on the ceiling at a greater angle.

Torpedo

Use the same principles here as you did for the crawl, but now it will be done on the back. You may have to teach some breath control to your swimmers to avoid their sniffing water through the nose. Having them exhale slowly through their noses will usually avoid this problem. Puffing up the upper lip under the nose will help to control a slow exhalation.

Torpedo kicking for short distances underwater follows torpedo push-offs. Consider this as an important drill in backstroke, because it teaches streamlining and a feel of water by the entire body. Swimmers should kick shallow and fast right off the wall and then build into a normal kicking range.

Streamlined Lateral Kicking

As in crawl, this kicking drill is done in a lateral position but on the back. Extend one arm back, keeping the other at the opposite side of the body. The extended arm is on the lower side of the body. Spear the arm as straight as possible, with the little finger and the elbow rotated inward toward the head.

Holding the arm in this spear position is fundamental for the success of this drill. Rotating the little finger and elbow inward and holding the arm in a straight spear position throughout the number of kicks on each side is essential. Do not permit your swimmers to bend their elbow or let the back of the hand rest on the water in this drill.

Have your swimmers practice on one side first, then the other. Correlate this drill to those of crawl streamlined lateral kicking. The 12/12, 10/10, 8/8, and 6/6 combination drills relate to backstroke as well as they do to crawl.

Surface Back Torpedo Kick

Swimmers should maintain a fully streamlined torpedo position on the back with both arms extended back behind the head, keeping the elbows straight and in tight behind the ears throughout the kicking set. Swimmers should hold their fingers in an elevated position slightly off the water. This will put your swimmers' feet at the proper kicking depth for backstroke and will also require them to kick with more force.

This is a good drill for emphasizing full stretch streamlining and for backstroke speed kicking. However, it doesn't permit swimmers to rotate the body while kicking as it is actually done in the backstroke.

One-Arm Swims

One-arm swims with one arm at the side are building blocks to full stroke swimming. Have a body-length mirror secured to the deck wall at the end of the pool. Backstrokers can learn quickly by watching themselves for a few strokes as they swim away from the mirror.

One-arm-build swims would include first adding a shoulder and hand lift just out of the water as the stroking arm enters. Make your next step a drill that lifts the shoulder and arm a quarter into the recovery, and then add lifting half into the recovery. Your swimmers should then be ready for the full backstroking arm cycle.

Other one-arm combinations that can help your swimmers achieve the backstroking rhythm would include 3/3, 2/2, and then 1/1 or regular backstroking cycle. In this drill, your swimmers perform three strokes with the right arm, then three with the left, two strokes with the right, then two with the left, and then finally, they swim the regular backstroke. Variations of this drill would be uneven stroking numbers such as 3/1, 2/1, 1/1, 1/2, 1/3, and so forth.

Touch Down

Consider the touch down backstroke drill a necessity to teach good rotation. This drill should start like a basic kicking drill—from a position of both arms at the sides of the legs. Swimmers should stroke one arm through the full range of motion and wait for it to get all the way back to the side of the leg before starting the other armstroke. Continue to repeat this sequence emphasizing body rotation (see Figure 9.8).

Break Water

Once touch down swims are being done correctly, add the break water drill. You should also add Han's Paddles to the break water drill once the skill level is acceptable.

Use the break water drill to teach both the armsweeps in backstroke and the acceleration of the arms within the arm pull. Swimmers should break water with the hand as it

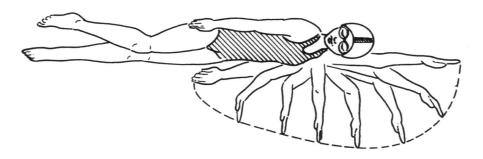

Figure 9.8

comes partially out of the water at the transition from the upsweep into the downsweep. Breaking water occurs at the peak of the upsweep in midpull, and the hand naturally accelerates as it meets less water resistance. This acceleration in the armstroke carries over into a faster downsweep as well.

Once you have taught the break water skill, use Han's Paddles most of the time. Your swimmers will feel more water with these holed paddles, and you can better see if the hand is at its most effective position when it breaks water. Look for about a quarter to a third of the paddle to break water. The paddle should break water so that it is almost evenly exposed out of the water. The top of the exposed paddle should be about even on both sides. Avoid any major angle at the exposed edge. This will help each swimmer attain a good bend in the arm at midpull.

👓 MIRROR, MIRROR ON THE WALL

I designed the break water drill in our practice sessions, and then I tried to teach it effectively. Using a wall mirror made it easy to teach. The mirror is essential in teaching the break water drill, because swimmers can teach themselves by watching their strokes in the mirror. Your swimmers can see if their paddle is breaking out of the water, and they can adjust their stroke to get it through the water surface sufficiently. You can use the mirror in any of the backstroke drills.

The break water drill can be used very effectively in the touch down drill, swimming, and back pulling. Back pull should be done with just a large rubber band around the ankles and no flotation devices. Pulling in this manner will help your backstrokers learn to effectively hold water through each stroking arm and to rotate properly to keep the body skewered in a streamlined position.

Back–Crawl Changeover

This essential backstroke drill is designed to teach your backstrokers how to roll and to maximize their distance per stroke, as well as how to feel the value of the maximum effective body rotation. It also helps backstroke swimmers adjust to the feel of rolling over to the front for the flip turn.

I teach a number of combinations for this drill. The 7/7 consists of seven strokes of crawl, then rolling into seven strokes of backstroke without any hesitation or loss of rhythm. A 5/5 involves five strokes of crawl and then rolling into five strokes of backstroke. The 3/3 is the fewest number of strokes that I teach. Combining the 7/7, 5/5, and 3/3 is another method of doing this drill.

Han's Paddles should be used frequently for this drill, because they maximize the distance per stroke from the rollover and help swimmers feel what is happening. With more mature swimmers, Grippers can also be used effectively.

Stop and Go

The stop and go drill, also essential in teaching backstroke, places great emphasis on strong legs, which are an advantage for great backstroke swimming. This drill helps develop in your swimmers good body roll, arm-sweeps, and the rifle barrel recovery. Make sure your swimmers do the backstroke so that each arm stops and holds at the 90° angle of the arm recovery. Each arm should stop at the peak of the arm recovery; that is, at the halfway mark in the recovery.

One arm strokes all the way through and stops at a hold position halfway through the recovery. When the moving arm reaches the same halfway stopping point or, in other words, draws even with the fixed arm, the fixed arm can then continue its stroke all the way through and back to this same point in the recovery. Continue to repeat this cycle on each arm.

Swimmers will have to use their legs in this stop and go drill, because holding one arm in this fixed overhead position will always require an honest effort from their kick. Reaching high at the fixed arm position also requires swimmers to elevate the shoulder of that arm partially out of the water, and this helps to get the body roll to the side of the opposite arm on entry.

Sculling

Continue to use the front-extended breaststroke position for sculling, as taught in the crawl. This position teaches the basic fundamentals of sculling for all four competitive strokes and also strengthens and conditions the muscles most used in effective sculling.

Your swimmers can also scull at the catch, midpull, and finish positions in backstroke. Isolate these positions, and have your swimmers scull at them for assigned distances. You can teach your backstrokers to scull the midpull or the finish position with both arms simultaneously. This creates more momentum, and swimmers get two for one, in that they use both arms simultaneously. In this drill swimmers will not duplicate the backstroke body position exactly, but that is not important. Swimmers will have to do the catch position scull, isolating one arm at a time, to simulate the actual stroke.

As recommended for the crawl, your swimmers should use Grippers on these backstroke sculling drills, because these aids will hold more water and help swimmers get the feel of the sculling action. The sculling for the finish in backstroke should be with the hands or Grippers facing the side of the legs and not the bottom of the pool. This is the final upsweep position in backstroke.

Spin Out

This is a drill that I would use for swimmers with special needs. Swimmers sit up in the water like they would in a small bathtub and raise the head up enough so that the water is at the back of the neck (see Figure 9.9). From this position, they stroke as fast as they can, swinging their arms rapidly back into the water after each stroke. This position will not maximize distance per stroke.

Figure 9.9

This drill can correct a lateral arm recovery and any tendency to cross behind the 12 o'clock entry position.

Double Arm Recovery

In this drill, also used for special situations, swimmers recover both arms at the same time. Because the body cannot rotate and

remain flat on the water in the double arm recovery, I don't use it often. However, it can help to attain a vertical arm recovery and a proper entry position. For example, your swimmers can't cross behind the 12 o'clock entry position in this drill (see Figure 9.10).

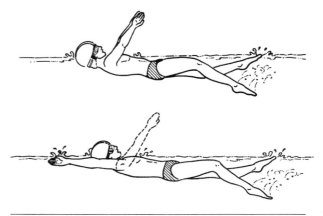

Figure 9.10

Swim the Rope

The swim the rope drill can be used in backstroke as it was in crawl. Anchor your rope as indicated in chapter 8. Your athletes should swim along one side of the rope and pull themselves past the point where they grab and hold the rope. They can use the arm on the side of the rope within any one length of swimming. This drill teaches how to attain maximum distance per stroke and the feeling of moving the body past the arm on the stroke.

I use swim the rope less than I once did, because I have added those many other drills that I have already outlined. Consider this drill a good backup for distance per stroke but secondary to those that I have already listed as essential.

Head Balance

Either backstroke swimming itself or backstroke drills with a plastic pocket coin purse balanced on the swimmers' forehead will eliminate excessive head roll. Use this drill to teach a stable head and eye position. I always carry a pocket coin purse for this purpose.

One-Arm Carry

A supplementary drill for your swimmers, the one-arm carry drill, will help strengthen the legs for great backstroke and will teach your swimmers to hold water effectively throughout the armstroke. Swimmers should backstroke with one arm while holding the other in a vertical 90° position. Your swimmers will kick and stroke effectively in order to keep their faces above water throughout this drill.

Summary

The following teaching and coaching hints will make fast backstroke swimming a reality for your swimmers:

1. Teach the backstroke in a similar manner to crawl.
2. Teach a back butterfly kick for use off the wall in the start and turns.
3. Make sure your swimmer's body rotates on a skewer in backstroke, as well as crawl.
4. Include in your sculling sweeps the following sequence of motions: down, up, down, up in four sweeps.
5. Teach the kick first in backstroke.
6. Employ a rifle barrel recovery.
7. Teach a thumb first exit into the recovery.
8. Use a little finger entry.
9. Ensure that your swimmers' head position is on the bow wave.
10. Teach your swimmers to enter at a position slightly short of 12 o'clock.
11. Employ the roll turn in your training.
12. Instruct your swimmers to stretch to the side when touching the wall at the finish.
13. Emphasize the torpedo position early in backstroke.
14. Teach lateral streamlined kicking as it is actually done in backstroke.
15. Utilize a wall mirror when teaching backstroke.
16. Employ Han's Paddles to teach the break water drill.
17. Remember the importance of sculling drills to the backstroke swimmer.
18. Combine back and crawl changeovers to emphasize body rotation.

Chapter 10

Teaching the Breaststroke

Breaststroke was the first competitive swimming stroke. The first successful crossing of the English Channel was done in breaststroke. This stroke has changed more during my coaching career than any other. The rules that govern it, too, have changed several times. Breaststroke is the slowest of the four competitive strokes, because the swimmer encounters more frontal resistance in it than in any of the others. It is the only stroke in which the arms and legs remain in or almost in the water throughout its entirety. There are many style variations in breaststroke, but the basic principles are the same.

Stroke Mechanics

In breaststroke, when your swimmers leave each wall, their arms start first. It is unique to the other competitive strokes in this regard. In all styles of breaststroke, swimmers pull with their arms first and then kick during the final part of the arm recovery.

We presently have two major styles of breaststroke, commonly called the "flat" and the "wave." Your philosophy of teaching breaststroke should be to get the most propulsion possible out of the arms and the legs with the least amount of frontal resistance. You also want to develop a flowing rhythm to the swimmer's stroke. This is true for whichever style your swimmers use, so permit them to develop the style best suited for them.

The flat style is characterized by the swimmer holding a nearly horizontal body position throughout the stroke. The shoulders remain underwater or nearly so, and the swimmer breathes by lifting and lowering the head, which also helps maintain the horizontal body position (see Figure 10.1).

Figure 10.1   The flat style breaststroke position.

Figure 10.2   The wave style breaststroke position.

In the wave style, the swimmer follows the angle of a wave, and his or her head and shoulders come up out of the water when breathing (see Figure 10.2).

The other phases of the two styles are very similar. I prefer to teach the wave style and then let my swimmers adapt to the style that appears to be the best fit. At present, I have more wave breaststroke swimmers, but I also have those who prefer the flat style. Tacoma Swim Club's last national champion, Bob Jackson, used the flat breaststroke style, and I never considered changing it, because I knew it was the best style for him.

Flat breaststroke swimmers tend to be very strong with stocky builds. Bob Jackson was a very good college football player with that type of build. On the other hand, wave breaststroke swimmers have a tendency to be less stocky and to have a more streamlined build. I don't know if body type effectively determines swim style; rather, it is just a general observation of mine that could change with my next great breaststroke swimmer.

The wave style appears to take greater advantage of the arm's forward lunge and seems to decrease some frontal resistance by breaking the shoulders free of the water.

However, this advantage may be offset by the slightly increased depth of the hips.

Technical Aspects

The armstroke for both the wave and flat breaststroke has two sweeps—an out- and an insweep before the recovery. On the insweep there is some upward sculling. Teach your swimmers to scull out and in. Breaststroke has the fewest armsweeps of the four competitive strokes.

Emphasize the following points regardless of which style of breaststroke you are teaching:

1. Hold water in the hands, forearms, and feet.
2. The toes hold water in a maximum flexed position as long as possible through the kick; follow through from the flexed position at the end of the kick only.
3. Keep the eye position somewhat fixed to avoid any major head and eye movement.
4. The swimmer's head drops back into the water as he or she attains the full forward arm extension.
5. Swimmers do most of their kicking in breaststroke.

The Wave

The outsweep should be fairly wide, and the hand should be pitched considerably more than in the crawl and butterfly (see Figure 10.3).

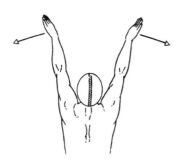

Figure 10.3 Hand pitch during the outsweep phase.

On the outsweep, the body is flat, and the elbows lock with the palms pitched out. Swimmers should not pull past the shoulders, and they must keep the arms at the water surface with the head in the water (see Figure 10.4).

Teach your swimmers to hold water on the insweep. The insweep is very fast, and the hands and elbows start forward during the insweep. The hands press toward each other on the insweep to facilitate the recovery. During the rotation from the out- to insweep, the elbows are bent and set high with the hands deeper in the water. The shoulders should still be in the water at the start of the insweep. The body is in a straight line at this position in the stroke (see Figure 10.5).

The head begins to come up during the in-scull, and the hands and shoulders are moving forward. Swimmers shouldn't raise the head too early. They should arch the back some to slide out and through the water in preparation for the lunge forward on the recovery. The elbows are under the shoulders in preparation for the lunge. The head is in line with the back so as to appear to be an extension of the back (see Figure 10.6).

You should be able to see daylight under the armpits of the swimmers at the peak of the wave. They should "hunch up" at the shoulders and elbows in preparation to lunge forward through a small hole. The shoulders shrug to the ears, and the elbows are under the shoulders; don't let them come together or touch each other (see Figure 10.7).

Have your swimmers blow air out, finishing their exhalation as the head lifts. They should breathe just after they finish the exhalation. At the peak of the lift, their eyes look forward and down.

Teach your swimmers to reenter by lunging forward over the water with the upper

Figure 10.4 The elbows-back position of the outsweep phase of the breaststroke.

Figure 10.5 The start position for the insweep phase.

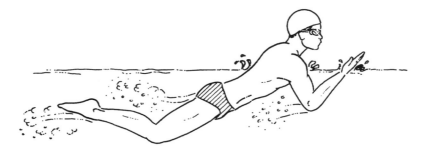

Figure 10.6 The head and back alignment.

Figure 10.7 The shoulder hunch position.

body. The head and shoulders should move forward and not down. Have them use their full body on the lunge. The head, back, and hips should be aligned during reentry (see Figure 10.8).

As the hands start forward, the heels begin to come up. The knees should only be as wide as the hips on the leg recovery. The heels are drawn up somewhat slowly without much effort. Your swimmers' knees are barely under the hip line, and the heels draw up toward the surface and the buttocks. This action reduces the angle at the hip joint, and as a result, frontal resistance is minimal.

At the catch position, have your swimmers point their feet out before kicking.

Your swimmers should explode through the full kicking range and close the kick, even to the point of having the soles of the feet together wherever possible.

The longer the feet are together, the more it decreases the resistance during the armstroke. Through the lunge, the hands are on the surface and may even come out of the water. This is acceptable and may be an advantage to some swimmers in accelerating their lunge forward. The hands and elbows are in line to start the lunge.

Have your swimmers get through the insweep and the shoulder hunch before they lunge forward. They need to get a full reach as they start down again over the wave. The kick finishes on the full forward extension. As the swimmers finish the kick, they need to start an outsweep for the next stroke cycle (see Figure 10.9).

Figure 10.8 The body position for reentry.

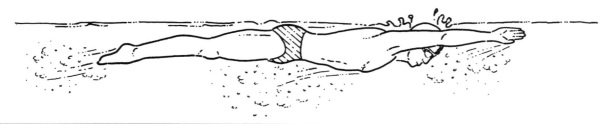

Figure 10.9 The body should be fully extended at the end of the kick and beginning of the next stroke.

Flat Breaststroke

The body position in the flat breaststroke style should be kept as horizontal as possible. The stroking action should take your swimmers forward between two points in as much of a straight line as possible. The flat style attempts to keep the up and down lifts much smaller than in that of the wave. There will always be some lift in the head and shoulders as a natural result of the armsweeps, but it is minimal.

Every great breaststroke swimmer has a strong kick. The position of the heels varies, but they should be no wider than the hips when coming up on their recovery. When delivering the kick, the feet turn out and accelerate through as wide an arch as the swimmer can attain. There must be a feeling of strength and continued acceleration throughout the total movement toward a streamlined position. At the completion of the kick, the feet are together and as close to the surface of the water as possible, bringing the swimmer back to the full body streamlining already discussed.

In the flat style, the arms pull from a fully extended and stretched position in front. The hands, trying to pull wide and not deep, are pitched out with the thumbs down. As the hands sweep out and down, the elbows are kept up with the hands rapidly swept together on the insweep. This action gives an upward lift of the shoulders, and then the swimmer takes a breath. The principles described here for the arms and legs in the flat style are also basically the same in that of the wave.

Sequence of Teaching Breaststroke

If you teach the crawlstroke first, which I recommend, you can build upon what you have already taught to help in training for the breaststroke. The breaststroke style of sculling with the arms extended out front is already in place, so use it as a starting position from which you can gradually increase the scull width through the full range of the breaststroke pull.

Once the sculling drill has been expanded into a breaststroke pull, you should introduce the breaststroke kick. Teach the kick first, and then you can build on its power. You may need to be a mechanic with some

of your swimmers, moving their legs manually to show them what's within the rules.

Timing the arms and legs should come next. Use the following sequence: pull (out and in), lunge forward, and then kick. Teach breathing next and then add it to your timing drills in the following order: pull out, in, breath, lunge, and then kick.

Breaststroke Starts, Turns, and Finishes

The need to teach and to practice starts, turns, and finishes can't be emphasized enough. Swimmers will frequently ask, "When are we going to practice turns?" You need to remind them that they *are* practicing turns every time they make one in the training session. The same is true for finishes. Every time they touch the wall at the completion of each repeat swim in practice, your swimmers are finishing a race. On occasion, you will practice starts on dive sprints or repeats.

Make your practice opportunities count toward always doing great starts, turns, and finishes. In addition, you will need to set aside a special time for some start, turn, and finish drills. This provides a great opportunity to teach and review the basics in these three invaluable areas.

Breaststroke Starts

The basics for the breaststroke start were outlined in chapter 8. The front start information applies to all of the competitive strokes with the exception of backstroke. There are some special considerations that are unique to the breaststroke starts, because rules permit one full underwater arm pull and kick before being required to surface sometime during the second armstroke. The one underwater armstroke allowed should be a full pull through, from the extended position out front, to an extended position back on or next to the legs.

Swimmers should set the elbows very high on the underwater pullout, with their hands in under their stomach. They should tuck the shoulders high into the ears at the end of the underwater pull (see Figure 10.10). This hunching action helps to minimize the

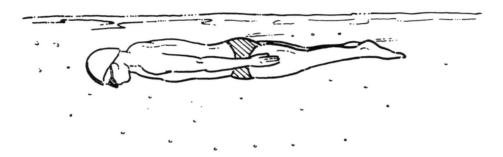

Figure 10.10   Hunching the shoulders at the finish of the underwater pull.

frontal resistance by reducing the eddies between the head and the shoulders.

Swimmers streamline their bodies by keeping their stomach and buttocks in tight and their feet together with the toes pointed. Swimmers should recover their hands close to the body, with the elbows in at their sides (see Figure 10.11).

Have your swimmers start their first pull over after the legs finish the kick. They should snap the feet together and then pull. The first surface stroke starts while the head is still a couple of inches underwater, and it should pop the swimmer through the surface tension. Make that first surface stroke their strongest. They should break with good momentum and then get into their racing stroke rhythm.

THE NATURAL

A gifted few swimmers have such great power in their legs that they can make their starts exceptionally good. Steve Lundquist, the 1984 Olympic 100-m breaststroke champion and world record holder, was one of these. In 1978, he was on the U.S. swimming national team that went to Taiwan for competition. Steve was still in high school at the time, and I was the coach of the team.

Steve's starts were so much better than any of the other competitors' that they attracted most of the media attention. As the meet progressed, a crowd formed at the side of the pool's starting end just to watch Steve get a 5 or 6 ft lead from his dive.

Turns

Your swimmers must learn to judge the walls by knowing where the wall is in relation to their stroke from about 10 ft out. Emphasize acceleration into the wall over the last 20 ft. It is very important that your swimmers accelerate their last stroke going into the wall, so that they can get high up on it for the breaststroke turn. They should avoid coming up to the wall off of a glide on the last stroke, because this will slow their turns.

When turning, swimmers should make the touch on the wall just short of their full arm extension. This will allow them to get their feet on the wall faster and to react quicker with their arms to give themselves a faster turn. The lead hand releases from the wall on contact, with the elbow down. The other hand grips or pushes, depending on whether the wall is flat or has a gutter to assist in getting the legs to the wall. Swimmers should

Figure 10.11   The recovery position at pull out.

drive their knees into their chest as quickly as possible. The elbow of the first arm off the wall goes down quickly, with the hand facing upward toward the ceiling. Swimmers should use this hand to scoop water up quickly, because it will get their legs on the wall faster. The feet should be crossed, one on top of the other, to help bring them to the wall through one hole in the water and not two. This action will help the swimmer get to the wall quicker.

The second hand off the wall comes close to the ear for the push-off. Your swimmers should go in and come out through the same hole in the water that they made going into the wall. The eye position should be on the turning point of the wall going in, and then it should move to the vertical as the second arm comes off the wall. This will help your swimmers get in and out through one hole. Extend the entire body into a streamlined position off the wall and then go into the

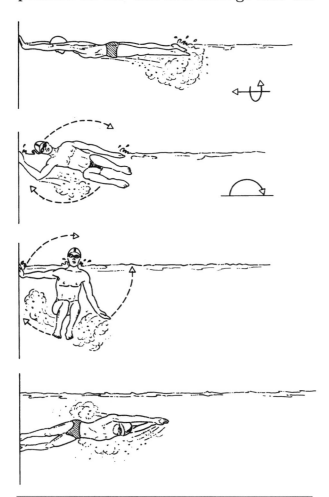

Figure 10.12 The four steps in teaching the breaststroke turn.

underwater stroke and the breakout as indicated in the start section (see Figure 10.12).

Finishes

Teach your swimmers to finish their breaststroke races with both arms fully extended on the surface and with the faces and eyes looking down in the water. Your swimmers' body should be in one straight line. They should make a determined lunge on their final stroke to get their hands on the wall as fast as possible. Provide special time for swimmers to practice this skill.

Special Tips for Teaching the Breaststroke

Teach and use drills to help your swimmers attain good breaststroke technique, following the same procedures outlined previously in this book. Explain, demonstrate, and then have your swimmers practice until they learn the technique. Expect the best from swimmers in their drill work, and praise them when they do well.

Maximum Distance Per Stroke

Use these drills and the minimum-number drills in the same manner as in the other strokes. Streamline kicking drills, the slide-kick drill, and one-arm swims with one arm extended will all promote maximum distance per stroke. Swimming with Grippers will also help your swimmers here. Counting the number of strokes per length is also important in developing your swimmers' maximum distance.

Feel of the Water

Occasionally, your athletes should swim with fists only, as indicated for the other strokes. The other feel of the water drills outlined for the crawl in chapter 8 can also be applied to the breaststroke.

Distance and Endurance Considerations

The longest competitive distance in breaststroke is the 200 (yards or meters). Breaststroke swimmers should concentrate on the legs in the first 100 and build the arms during the second. Swimmers use the first three strokes after the dive and breakout to get into the rhythm of the stroke. Athletes should swim fast but with little effort through the first 50, and make certain that they are stretching out on the stroke. The second 50 should be as economical as possible, but when going into the turn at the 100, your swimmers should build their speed for the last three strokes.

In the third 50, swimmers must establish an armstroke rhythm that they can handle and that can place them at their best competitive position in the race. Athletes should hold or increase their stroking tempo through the final 50 and focus on their technique as they begin to tire. On the finish, swimmers must concentrate on the final wall as they close in.

Drills for Breaststroke

I'm listing the major drills that I use to teach this stroke, as well as some of those that won't be necessary for every swimmer. You will find that some drills suit your teaching style better than others. Whatever the case may be, be the captain of your own ship, but teach technique, because fast breaststroke swimming is the result of good stroke technique.

Sculling

Review the breaststroke sculling position—the front extended position—as you taught it in the crawl. In sculling, your swimmers' hands are high on the water close to the surface. Using Grippers will enhance the feel of sculling for your swimmers who are about 12 years and older. I don't use Grippers for the younger swimmers.

The in-scull position should also be taught and practiced but not first in the sculling sequence. I prefer that swimmers learn some additional breaststroke skills before adding this one. This in-scull drill should be done with swimmers on their front in a horizontal position with the face in or out of the water. In-scull from the position of the arms at the end of their lateral outsweep.

Another more advanced drill is vertical in-sculling. Swimmers take a vertical or standing position in deep water and use only their arms. The in-scull movement, also called the "wipe the bowl drill," consists of pressing the hands out a short distance and then sculling in fast. Swimmers press outward to the sides of an imaginary bowl and then down and in along its sides. The in-sculling will lift them vertically in the water, and the power generated by the insweep becomes obvious to swimmers. Use Grippers on these in-scull drills as you did on that for the out-scull.

From Sculling to Breaststroke Pull

Gradually build the extended sculling drill to a full armstroke by using a standing drill in front of the mirror. The walking drill can help teach swimmers to move their body forward on the armstroke. Use such a drill to move swimmers into a few basic breaststroke arm pulls, with their faces in the water and their legs extended behind them. Have them walk and then push off the bottom and glide forward into this position.

Wall Kick

Teach the wall kick first by having swimmers grip the gutter with both hands and going through the movements of the breaststroke kick. With some of your swimmers, you will have to do this by manually working their feet.

Arms Extended, Streamlined Kicking

Next, teach swimmers to kick breaststroke in the streamlined position with both their arms extended out front and with their faces in the water. Have swimmers do this for short distances above and below the surface of the water.

Launching Drill

After the streamlined, arms-extended kicking position, I teach the launching drill to my breaststrokers. Swimmers must stand in water from waist- to shoulder-depth with their backs braced against the pool wall. Your swimmer should be facing away from you in the frontal-extended arm position. Place each foot of the swimmer into each of your hands. Hold the feet so that you are

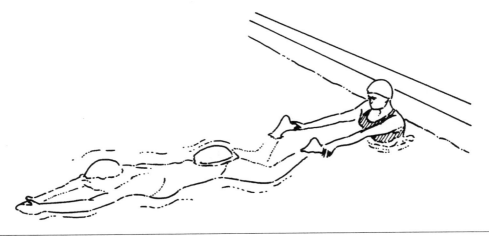

Figure 10.13

exerting hand pressure on the swimmer's soles. Straighten your elbows, and then have the swimmer kick back against your braced arms to be launched forward through the water (see Figure 10.13).

Off the force of the kick, the swimmer learns the feel of moving forward, and you can keep the swimmer's toes flexed out with your hands to enforce good technique. I have the swimmers continue to kick across the pool on their own after being launched.

Eggbeater Kick

Alternating the breaststroke kick from one leg to the other is called the eggbeater kick. This drill helps swimmers attain the flexed toe position so necessary for their success, and it can be done in the streamlined kicking position or on a kickboard. I prefer doing this drill and most of all the kicking without a kickboard.

Arms-Back Kicking

Have your swimmers lock their thumbs behind the back and as low on the hips as the length of their arms permits. Your swimmers should be on their front. Have them draw their heels up until they touch their fingertips, before they turn their feet out for the kick. This action teaches swimmers to bring their heels up behind the buttocks correctly and eliminates the problem of their bringing the knees under the body too much in the recovery. Swimmers should kick with the head out of the water and the shoulders at water level.

Vertical Kicking

Have your swimmers stand in deep water and kick vertically. Breaststrokers can strengthen their kick with this drill, especially when they lift their arms overhead and out of the water. For the more advanced swimmers, adding weights also helps. Because it decreases the full range of the kicking motion, vertical kicking is a supplementary drill. It requires a nearly continuous kicking action, but it does stress the legs and forces an accelerating kicking movement.

Back Breaststroke Kick

Kicking breaststroke on the back is a supplementary method of improving your swimmers' feel for the kicking movements. When doing this drill, swimmers must keep both arms in the streamlined torpedo position behind their heads.

Kick With a Pull Buoy

Kicking breaststroke with a pull buoy between the thighs will help some of your swimmers correct their kicking recovery and will encourage more from their flexed toes on the kick itself.

Slide-Kick Drill

This drill is designed to teach the timing of the arms and legs in breaststroke. Swimmers start from the streamlined kicking position on the front. One hand should be locked over the other and in this locked position, the hands slide to the top of the head. The elbows will have to bend to permit this slide of the hands to the head, and the swimmer shouldn't kick during this motion.

Once the hands touch the head, the swimmer lunges forward and kicks. The swimmer must stretch at the completion of the kick before starting the slide of the hands again. At the beginning, have swimmers do only a few strokes without breathing over short distances. As an advanced technique, you can add breathing to this drill in the following sequence: slide, breathe, lunge, and kick.

Pulling With the Head Up

In this drill, swimmers pull with the head up out of the water and with the chin riding on the water surface. Don't use any leg flotation devices in this drill. This teaches swimmers to hold water through both armsweeps and helps to keep their hands on the water through the stroke. Where appropriate, use Grippers for some of this pulling.

Inner Tube Pulling

Some swimmers may benefit from pulling within an inner tube. If you have swimmers pulling their elbows back behind the shoulder line, place them into a passenger-car-sized inner tube. The inner tube should rest under their armpits. As they pull breaststroke from this position, the swimmers' arms will bump the inner tube before they can get too far back in the stroke. This self-teaching method reminds the swimmer when to sweep the arms in.

Swim Under the Rope

Stretch a rope over the water from one end of the pool to the other, preferably over the tops of the starting blocks at the pool's opposite ends. Have your swimmers do the breaststroke under this rope. They should attempt to get enough lift from their insweep to bounce the rope with their head. This power drill for the insweep can help your swimmers feel the wave action.

One-Arm Swims

One-arm swims can be done two ways. One method, swimming one-arm breaststroke with one arm extended out front, helps to lengthen the stroke and to maximize the distance per stroke. Have your swimmers keep their forward arm fully extended like a spear. The other method of doing the one-arm breaststroke drill, keeping one arm back at the side, can be used to help some swimmers reduce the amount of their glide. I seldom use the second method.

Variation Drills

Many of the variation drills are essential for every swimmer. Swimming and kicking breaststroke underwater will assist your swimmers to get a better feel for the stroke and will teach them explosive breathing when they surface.

For a good variation drill, have your swimmers kick three on the surface in the extended, streamlined arm position and then have them dive underwater and kick two or three according to their ability level. Or you can have them swim three on the surface and then dive underwater and swim two or three strokes in the regular surface style. Some pulling can be done this same way. These variations can be expanded to three kicks up, two kicks underwater, three swims up, two swims underwater, three pulls up, two pulls underwater.

Breaststroke With Dolphin Kick

This drill can help swimmers to feel the rhythm and to have an explosive lunge in breaststroke. Have them use the dolphin kick at the same position in the stroke in which they would normally use the breaststroke kick. Using fins in this drill can also be a valuable addition.

Underwater Pull-Out Drill

Use underwater pull-outs for more than one stroke in some of your training swims. Have your swimmers take two underwater pull-out strokes off of some walls if it's within their abilities. This drill strengthens your swimmers' control over their breathing and makes their taking the one allowed underwater stroke much easier in competition.

Summary

Use these guidelines to help your swimmers attain the technique and subsequent speed necessary for success in breaststroke swimming:

1. The basic fundamentals are the same in both the wave and flat styles of breaststroke.
2. Don't change a winning style.
3. Teach a wide outsweep.
4. Don't let your swimmers pull past the shoulders.
5. Swimmers must continue to hold water on the insweep.
6. Your swimmers should lunge forward on the recovery.
7. Swimmers must exhale on the head lift.
8. At the peak of the lift, swimmers should look forward and down with their eyes.
9. After the lunge, swimmers must hold their head, back, and hips in line.
10. On leg recovery, the knees should be no wider than the hips, the feet should be drawn up slowly, and the heels should be drawn up toward the buttocks.
11. Swimmers should flex the toes out through the delivery of the kick.
12. Most of your swimmers' kicking should be in breaststroke.
13. Build the swimmers' armstroke from your basic sculling drills.
14. Have your swimmers set their elbows high on the underwater pull-out.
15. Swimmers should hunch their shoulders at the completion of the underwater pull-out.
16. When touching the wall for the turn, your swimmers should be short of the full arm extension.
17. For fast turns, have your swimmers get their feet on the wall quickly.
18. Swimmers must finish with both arms fully extended.
19. Sculling drills are essential in the breaststroke.
20. Use drills to teach swimmers the breaststroke skills.

Chapter 11

Teaching the Butterfly

Butterfly became an official competitive stroke several years after I started coaching high school. Previously I had used a butterfly armstroke with a breaststroke kick within the old breaststroke rules. However, the new butterfly kick was somewhat of a mystery, and I made a lot of mistakes coaching it.

 SEE THE DOLPHINS SWIM

I can still remember watching a butterfly teaching movie that featured dolphins. These beautiful creatures made swimming look so easy with their full body undulation, and we tried to copy it in our teaching of the butterfly. But this proved to be one of our first major mistakes, because we tried to initiate the kick from the upper body instead of the hips.

The butterfly kick is essentially the same motion used in the crawl flutter kick. The distinguishing characteristic is that both legs kick in the same direction simultaneously.

This simultaneous kick forces the hips up at the completion of the downkick.

The butterfly armstroke is also done simultaneously, and the stroke is done on the front without body rotation, as in the crawl and backstroke. Sculling sweeps provide the "new" water necessary for maximizing distance per stroke.

Stroke Mechanics

Once again, consider the technique that you want to teach first; then use the sequence of skills that will teach it most effectively.

Technical Aspects

You will need to teach technique that maximizes propulsion and distance per stroke and minimizes resistance. Swimmers can learn the butterfly as easily as any other competitive stroke when you are confident in your teaching skills. You are the key.

Expect quality butterfly at all times in practice. Permitting the stroke to break down and then allowing swimmers to practice it imperfectly isn't recommended. There are five areas of consideration for your coaching: entry, sculling sweeps, recovery, kicking, and breathing.

Entry

Teach your swimmers to reach long on the entry. They will get good distance on their stroke by extending the arms and body on entry. Have them drive their chins down prior to the arm entry during the last half of the recovery. This will help them get their arms into the entry quickly and efficiently. Having the head up on the last half of the recovery will interfere with arm momentum into the entry.

It is very important that the back of the head and the end of the spine be lined up during this entry position. Swimmers should keep the chin down in the water and the head aligned with the spine. The chin is pressed down and forward, with that platform position held by stretching the chin and the chest down on entry. The eyes should focus down and slightly forward. Everything lands at once, and this brings the hips up on the water. The timing is to have the hips up high on the arm entry and the face down with the legs fully extended (see Figure 11.1).

I used to tell swimmers to throw the head to the chest just before the arm entry. This gave the necessary timing, but it also placed the head lower than the spine. Use some caution and adjust the head throw to allow swimmers more control and to keep their heads and spines aligned. This will give swimmers a longer body on the water in the best position to take advantage of the coming armstroke.

Water should cover the back of the head and spine after entry. There is an underwater portion to this stroke, and one of the best ways to see it is to watch swimmers upside-down: on the deck, bend over and watch them looking back under your armpit.

Butterfly swimmers should enter the water with arms about shoulder-width apart to eliminate some of the resistance encountered when arms are spread wider. It also permits a more continuous and fluid butterfly as the hands are in good position to start the armstroke. Entering with arms closer than shoulder-width may delay swimmers slightly in reaching the proper catch position.

Sculling Sweeps

Teach an outsweep, an insweep, and an upsweep. The outsweep sets up the stroke for the two later power sweeps. The hands

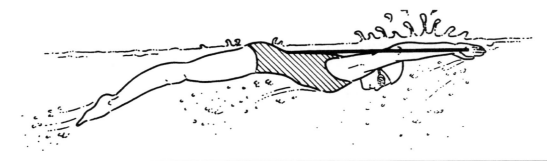

Figure 11.1 Body alignment for the butterfly entry.

Figure 11.2 Positioning for the outsweep phase.

are pitched outward in a controlled movement to gradually arrive at a good catch for the insweep (see Figure 11.2).

During the insweep, there is a downward and inward action. At one point on the insweep the swimmer sets the elbows in an up position and pushes the body over and past the elbows (see Figure 11.3). This propulsive sweep comes in under the body to a point where the hands are very close together.

Figure 11.3 Positioning for the insweep phase.

The upsweep starts from the position where the hands are close together under the body at the completion of the insweep. It is a propulsive sweep that moves out, back, and up (see Figure 11.4).

Figure 11.4 Positioning for the upsweep phase.

Recovery

In the armstroke recovery, swimmers should flex their elbows slightly. This will relax the arms more in the recovery and place the elbows in a slightly up position on the entry. The flexibility level of the swimmer will determine the ability to flex or bend the arm at the elbow; some swimmers will have to use a straight arm recovery.

In the butterfly recovery, the little finger is first to exit the water. Teach a "karate chop" finish and exit of the hands. The hands move outward in a ballistic action, and the palms are up on the first part of the recovery (see Figure 11.5). During the recovery, the palms rotate so that they face down during the recovery's second half. On entry, the palms are pitched out slightly.

Kicking

In order to keep the butterfly kick continuous and explosive, it must originate from the hips with flexible knees, as it does in the crawl. Although the simultaneous kicking action results in undulating hips, the kick must still originate from the hips and not higher in the body.

The depth of the kick will be in a greater range than in the crawl (see Figure 11.6). Body rotation in the crawl required a width and depth range within the kick. In the butterfly, only the depth is involved and it takes the kick to a slightly greater depth than in that of the crawl. The heels of the feet rise to the water surface on the up kick. The feet and legs come together on the down kick and spread slightly on the up kick.

Breathing

Teach swimmers to breathe late in the arm pull. They should begin to move the chin forward

Figure 11.5 Exiting with the little finger up during the recovery stage.

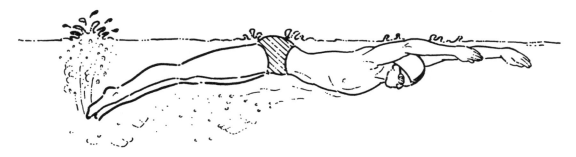

Figure 11.6 The proper depth for the butterfly kick.

toward the breathing position on the final upsweep of the arms and take the breath at the end of the upsweep or at the release and start of the recovery. This is the most efficient position in which to breathe, because the swimmer's shoulders are out of the water (see Figure 11.7).

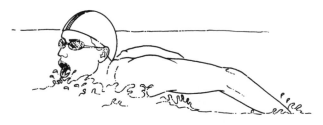

Figure 11.7 The best position for breathing is at the end of the upsweep and at the start of the recovery phases.

Teach swimmers to breathe on every second stroke, even though many great butterfly swimmers can breathe every stroke efficiently. You can sort this out later as your swimmers mature. The 200 butterfly races may require breathing every stroke for some swimmers to be successful. However, if you teach breathing every other stroke, you'll make many of the other skills easier to learn.

Sequence of Teaching Butterfly

I prefer to teach the armstroke first to create more excitement in the swimmers and to make it easier for them to master butterfly. You can teach the arms and legs almost simultaneously, but I prefer that swimmers feel they are actually swimming butterfly before I introduce the leg action. It is easier to add a continuous and explosive leg kick to an armstroke already in place than it is to do the reverse.

Teaching the butterfly from the legs can lead to a legs-dominated stroke with poor timing and breathing. Getting the arms into the recovery can also become a hangup, as well as the other added risk of having swimmers drop their elbows on entry. Teaching arms first avoids most of these problems.

My review of the torpedo position would come next, and then I would move immediately into the kicking drills. I would come back into the armstroke with a one-arm drill that would be built from the kicking drills. I would then work breathing drills into the one-arm drills, using an orderly and natural sequence. Finally, I could add any number of butterfly drills to maximize distance per stroke before introducing any timed swims.

Butterfly Starts, Turns, and Finishes

Follow my same recommendations for the other strokes. Teach and practice starts, turns, and finishes, because your swimmers will never get consistently fast unless you provide the necessary techniques and the time to practice them.

Butterfly Starts

The front start discussed in chapter 8 provides the basics for all front starts; however, there are some special considerations for the butterfly start. Before breaking out into the armstroke, swimmers must establish the

kick underwater with very quick and shallow butterfly kicks while streamlining in the torpedo position.

Don't permit your swimmers to breathe on the first arm pull. They can breathe on the second stroke or later depending on the distance of the race and their personal preference. On the first stroke, swimmers should exaggerate the wrist snap, or "karate chop" to finish off the underwater stroke and to get into the recovery. This exaggerated stroke, which is actually a little shorter than normal ones, helps the recovery and gets the stroke out in front of the body quickly. Stress a very clean or an "eye of the needle" entry on this first armstroke, because it requires great streamlining and maximizes the momentum swimmers receive from their start and into the early butterfly strokes.

Turns

The butterfly turn is the same as the breaststroke turn at the wall. (For specifics, refer to the turn section of chapter 10.) Once the push-off has been executed, the same special considerations that I have already indicated for the butterfly start apply to the turn. Judging the wall is critical for the success of the butterfly turn, as it is in the breaststroke.

The no-wall drill in midpool helps teach fast butterfly turns. Have your swimmers do three very fast strokes in midpool and then have them turn quickly without the wall.

Finishes

In the finish of butterfly races, the swimmers have both the arms fully extended on the surface and the head down, as it is in breaststroke. Swimmers shouldn't breathe from the backstroke flags to the finish of the race. Swimmers must judge the wall correctly, and when they are reasonably close to it, they should stretch and kick and lunge for the wall on the final stroke. Getting the hands on the wall fast is a learned skill, so swimmers must practice it.

 A GOLDEN TOUCH

I interviewed on video several of the finalists in the butterfly events at the 1992 Olympic Trials for my presentation at the American Swimming Coaches' Association World Clinic. Several months prior to the Olympic Games, Pablo Morales told me about all the time he spent practicing the butterfly race finish and about how he would focus on making a good finish when he was tired at the race's end. Pablo Morales won a very close 100-m butterfly race and the gold medal at Barcelona as a result of his practice.

Special Tips for Teaching the Butterfly

The sequence of the major training drills is important. Particularly in the case of butterfly, all drills must be done correctly, because butterfly swimmers suffer the most from poor technique. Good technique makes this stroke easy and, to me, makes it a work of art—there is beauty in good butterfly swimming, but there is the beast in bad butterfly technique. Nowhere is this more true than in butterfly.

Swimmers should practice in butterfly drills and swimming for distances within their skill level, because their stroke will break down if you overload them.

Maximum Distance Per Stroke

Maximum distance per stroke drills must be done in butterfly as they were done in the other strokes. Counting strokes per length is the basic drill. You must also use the minimum-number drill.

Feel of the Water

As in the other strokes, swimmers use the fists only in some of the butterfly. Using the fingers in the A-OK, index, and pinky signs is also good occasionally to attain a feel of the water.

Fins

I prefer to use the shortened fins that I have described in previous chapters for these kicking drills. Fins can be used in almost all of the kicking and swimming drills, but they have their greatest value in the former, especially the torpedo back dolphin kick above and underwater and the vertical kicking drills.

Paddle Swims

Use the Gripper on your more mature swimmers to help them set the stroke up correctly on entry. These paddles force the hands to position themselves efficiently on entry, because they will not stay on during a bad entry. The paddle's grooves hold and gather water on the hands and forearms for the best stroking position. Such a setup at the stroke's start maximizes the distance per stroke.

The Gripper teaches the necessity of acceleration through the back half of the armstroke, because when wearing it, swimmers have to pick up speed in the armstroke to effectively karate chop their hands into the recovery. The hands won't exit the water cleanly, unless the swimmers accelerate them at this point in the stroke. By using the Gripper, swimmers learn for themselves the method for developing a great back half in the butterfly armstroke.

I recommend using Han's Paddles in the short power swims. I use them almost exclusively in our power rack swims and often in short power bursts. I also use them in some of our race-pace swims to help swimmers maximize their distance per stroke.

Distance and Endurance Considerations

The racing distance in butterfly extends to 200 (yards or meters), which is not a long race. Some butterfly swimmers might argue that point but those who develop great butterfly technique can swim the 200 at least adequately.

A powerful leg kick is essential for success in the butterfly, particularly for the 100 butterfly swimmer. In the 200, swimmers may breathe more often than every two strokes to finish well. Sustained speed is more important in the 200, so the minimum-number drills are essential.

Drills for the Butterfly

Again I will list those drills that I consider to be essential and then some additional ones that may get the point across better to some of your swimmers. Always explain each skill, then demonstrate it correctly, and then have swimmers practice it within the particular drill you are teaching.

Basic Arms

If you can effectively reach and hold their arms through the full stroke, you should get into the water with your younger swimmers, stand behind them, and work their arms manually.

In front of a wall mirror, have your swimmers do the standing drill in waist-deep water. If you don't have a mirror, have them face you and duplicate the butterfly armstroke that you are doing on the pool deck. Fix and hold certain armstroke positions and talk them through each one.

1. Arms enter at shoulder width
2. Hands pitched out on entry with little finger higher than the thumb
3. Outsweep

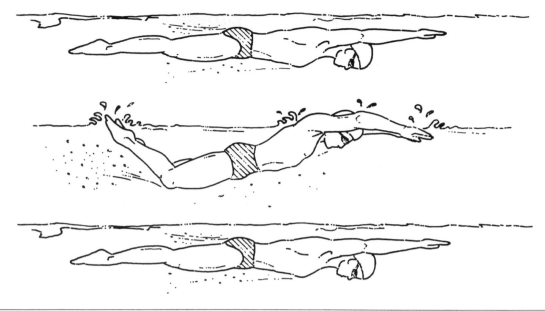

Figure 11.8

4. Insweep
5. Upsweep
6. Karate chop release
7. First half recovery
8. Midrecovery

Next swimmers should do the walking butterfly drill into and away from the mirror. Then move swimmers from the walking butterfly to one or two strokes of butterfly without breathing.

Torpedo or "Dead Man's" Butterfly

After you have taught the basic armstroke, proceed into the torpedo or "dead man's" butterfly. The torpedo butterfly is considered the basic position for the stroke. Have swimmers push off the wall for a review of the torpedo position used in crawl. Swimmers should be only one body-width under the surface when in the torpedo position.

Next, have them push off in this dead man's position and glide. When slowing down, the swimmer should scull out and take one armstroke and then dive back into the original torpedo position just under the surface (see Figure 11.8). Even if it is only one stroke, this is the butterfly. Swimmers should get their arms back into the water in the extended torpedo position quietly. They can then repeat a second stroke, after they again attain that torpedo or dead man's position.

Jumping Jack Butterfly

I use this drill for beginners. I don't consider it to be essential, but many coaches use it and young kids love to do it. In waist-deep water, the swimmer leaps off the bottom and dives through the surface, back underwater and then repeats the process.

Flutter to Butterfly Kick

Begin new swimmers with the crawl flutterkick and then move them to the butterfly kick. Have your swimmers review the front flutterkick by having them, on their front, hold onto the wall. Next, have them flutterkick only one leg at a time, explaining to them that this is also the same kick used in the one-leg butterfly. Progress from one-leg kicking to kicking butterfly by using both legs simultaneously.

Have your swimmers go through this same transition on a kickboard over short distances. They should move from flutterkick, to one-leg flutterkick, back to flutterkick, and then back to full butterfly kick. Finally, swimmers should progress to doing this drill in the torpedo position and without a kickboard.

Underwater Kick

For short distances under 20 ft, swimmers should torpedo butterfly kick off the wall on their front, back, and side. Underwater kicking is important for all levels of swimmers, and it teaches them to feel water on both sides of their legs when kicking. Changing from front to back and to the side enhances a swimmer's ability to learn how to move water effectively to maximize kick propulsion.

When swimmers are at an advanced level, you can have them push off the bottom of the pool's deep end and torpedo kick through the surface. This drill helps develop streamlining and an explosive kick. You may want to add a weight belt in this drill for your most advanced swimmers.

Surface Kicking

The back butterfly kick, which should always be taught with the body in the torpedo position and on the surface, is one of the most effective methods for swimmers to learn a continuous and quick dolphin kick through the actual butterfly swimming range. With this kick it is easier to be continuous and not hesitant at the completion of the up kick. I believe that all butterfly swimmers should do a high percentage of their kicking in back butterfly.

Practice the side butterfly kick on both sides, and make sure swimmers keep one arm forward. This drill helps swimmers develop a feel for water on both sides of their legs, because their legs don't catch surface air. This drill is used much less often than the back butterfly kick drill.

Swimmers should butterfly kick on the front as well with the arms extended forward and the head placed into the torpedo position. With the more advanced swimmers, have them hold the head up to develop more explosive power from their kick. They can also develop power by locking the thumbs behind the hips and kicking with the head held out of the water.

I prefer not to teach kicking with the kickboard. I use it only in drills that require an explosive kick and a major effort, like timed fast kicks. I also use a small ankle weight belt sometimes, which is helpful in getting the best out of kicking on a kickboard.

Kick sets must always be worked with an emphasis on quality. Bill Sweetenham, the great Australian coach, sets a goal for his swimmers

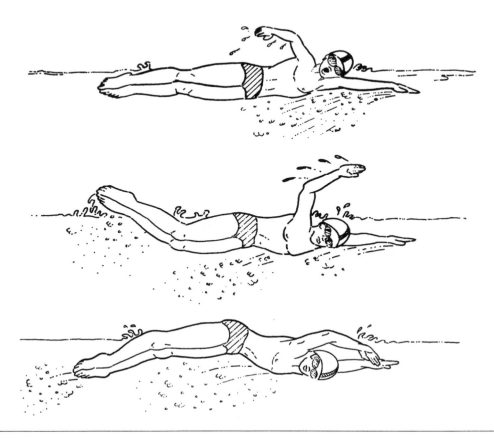

Figure 11.9

to kick 100 m within 20 s of their personal-best 100-m swimming time in butterfly.

Vertical Kicking

Teach your swimmers vertical butterfly kicking in deep water to develop power and a continuous explosive kick through the correct range. The swimmer's entire head and neck should be out of water during this drill. Add a weight belt for advanced swimmers.

One-Arm Swims With One Arm Extended

Variations of one-arm swims are the backbone of learning the butterfly, but the first step is to learn the one-arm butterfly with one arm extended. Through the full stroke cycle, the arm must be speared forward and fully extended with the little finger and elbow pitched slightly up. Breathe to the side in this drill, on the side of the stroking arm.

Breathing to the stroking-arm side automatically teaches the swimmer to breathe late in the pull. As the arm finishes the

stroke, the shoulder lifts and the chin can easily follow the shoulder to breathe (see Figure 11.9). Practice this drill on both sides.

The next step is to move from the one-arm stroke to the full stroke. I usually start with a 3/3/3 drill. My swimmers will do three one-arm butterfly strokes on the left side and breathe to the right, then swim three on the left side and breathe to the left, and then swim three full butterfly strokes and breathe forward every second stroke. This drill teaches the breathing timing and the rhythm of butterfly. Moving from side breathing to forward breathing establishes the late pattern for butterfly.

My next combined drill is a 1/1/1, a 1/1/2, a 1/1/3, and so on. Swimmers do one butterfly stroke on the right side, one on the left, and then one full butterfly stroke. Immediately they go back to one stroke on the right, one on the left, and two full butterfly strokes, and then so on, to whatever number of full strokes that you desire according to the swimmers' level.

Once swimmers learn these one-arm drills, you can improvise any challenging

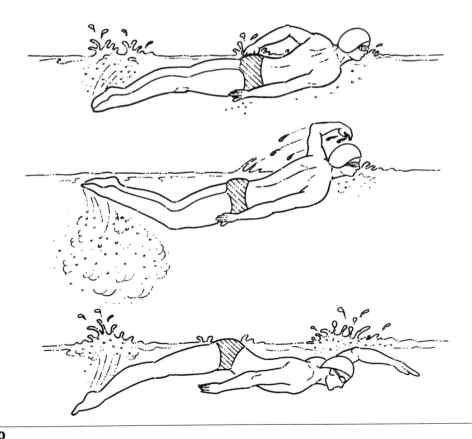

Figure 11.10

combination, like three right, two left, one right, three left. A good combination drill for your more advanced level swimmers would be three right, three full butterfly strokes with no breathing, three left, and three full strokes with no breathing. You are limited only by your own ingenuity.

Multiple Kick Butterfly

Also called the "lazy man's" butterfly, swimmers do the full stroke, but they kick three, four, or five or more kicks, with the arms speared out front, before they take their next stroke. This is a good kicking drill that delivers an explosive armstroke with less frequency than in normal butterfly, but it still helps swimmers develop breath control. I like to combine this multiple kicking drill with the torpedo back butterfly kick. For example, when swimming 50s, athletes do the first 25 in five-kick butterfly and the last in torpedo back butterfly kick.

Another good variation of this drill is to do four kicks underwater and then two explosive full strokes of swimming. Challenge your swimmers with new variations in these drills, but always demand perfect technique.

Extra Kicks Off Walls

Kicking five or more times off each wall before breaking out into the armstroke is a good drill to teach swimmers to use explosive kicking. Swimmers should streamline their bodies into a full torpedo position through all of these kicks. Extra kicks also help to establish the importance of the kick off every wall as the swimmer goes back into full butterfly stroking.

One-Arm Swims With One Arm at Side

In this drill, swimmers do one-arm butterfly with the nonstroking arm at the side (see Figure 11.10). This action will shorten the swimmer's stroke slightly and eliminate some of the pause out front on the entry. Swimmers who need to build their stroking tempo should use this drill. The current world record holder, Melvin Stewart, recommended this drill during those 1992 Olympic Trials' video interviews I did.

Sculling

As in all strokes, emphasize sculling. The sculling drills outlined in chapter 8 are essential in butterfly. Remember to use the Gripper in a high percentage of your sculling drills.

Transition Drills

Using a sequence of drills that combine and lead into the full stroke is a very efficient method of teaching in practice. One example might include: four kicks underwater on the front, four kicks right, and then regular stroking for the remainder of the repeat distance.

Speed Drill

In the torpedo position, swimmers kick six to eight fast power kicks underwater, and then break out with three very fast and full butterfly strokes before returning to regular pace. Another speed drill involves swimming short bursts—any distance from 10 to 20 yd, depending on the swimmer's ability—of no-breath sprints on longer rest and perfect stroke.

Summary

These are the guidelines for teaching and coaching great butterfly:

1. Teach and expect quality butterfly.
2. Begin training with the armstroke.
3. Swimmers should employ a little finger and a karate chop exit.
4. At the start of the recovery the swimmer's palms should be up.
5. On entry the swimmer's palms should be down and pitched out slightly.
6. Sculling skills are important in butterfly.
7. The swimmer should breathe late in the finish of the pull.
8. Swimmers must reach long on the entry.
9. The face must be down before the arms enter.
10. On entry, the back of the head and spine are aligned.
11. Butterfly should be partially done underwater.
12. A swimmer's entry should be near the shoulder tips.
13. Teach swimmers to breathe every second stroke.
14. Swimmers must not breathe from the backstroke flags to the wall at the finish.
15. Have swimmers practice butterfly only at distances that maintain quality technique.
16. Swimmers should kick a high percentage of butterfly in the torpedo back position.
17. Use the one-arm swim with one arm extended drills as the basis for teaching correct technique.
18. The Gripper teaches correct underwater armstroking technique.

Part IV

Coaching Meets

Chapter 12

Preparing for Meets

Vary the type of preparation for swim meets, because all of them aren't equally important. You have already used your master calendar to determine which meets are the highest priority. Your championship meet is the major one on which to maintain your focus.

Readying Your Team

Train your swimmers, providing them consistent stress levels throughout each week of the season according to plan. Do the sets scheduled for that day's master plan at the intensity level necessary to meet the objectives of the training categories explained in chapter 5. Make the championship meet your prime concern; all other meets must help prepare your swimmers to do their best at the championship.

Swimming is not like football, basketball, or many other team sports. In most sports, every game is important in order to make the playoffs or to win the league championship. Consequently, coaches of these sports cannot risk having their athletes too exhausted to compete at their best in the league competition.

On the other hand, the championship in swimming is usually decided at the championship meet. The team that scores the most points at that *one* competition wins. As a result, you need to train your athletes through most of the league meets in order to effectively taper and rest them for the final championship competition.

TOO MUCH TOO SOON!

Some high school and club teams swim fast in all or most of their regular season meets and

119

then fail at their championship. Every year that I have coached, I've seen this from some teams, and I've had it happen myself. I learned quickly that swimmers must have a consistent training program throughout the season that is focused on the championship meet. This was the only way that I could get high-level performances from my swimmers when we swam at the championship meet.

My high school team wasn't always seeded first going into the state championship meet. The top swimming times that are recorded during the regular dual meet season determine the rankings and the favorite team going into the championship meet. Our regular season swimming times may not have been the best, but our state championship times were at the top.

Too many coaches rest their teams too often during the season. Keep your ego under control and have confidence in your training calendar. I've seen too many coaches who wanted fast times from their swimmers too soon in the season. Be patient and take some risks in the regular season schedule, even if it means an unwelcome loss. The key is to be there when it counts most.

Types of Meets

There are several types of swim meets in a normal schedule, the championship being most often the final season meet.

Dual meets make up most of the schedule in high school and college swimming and are also used in club and YMCA swimming but less often. In club swimming, invitational meets make up most of the schedule, but they are also used in YMCA, high school, and college swimming. Invitational meets include at least several teams and are sometimes very large.

Preparing for Regular Season Meets

Prepare for the regular season meets as though they were another training session. I've heard the true expression, "Competition is the purest form of training." You can never duplicate racing conditions in training as you do in actual competition. You should consider competitive races as speed training for swimmers and as an opportunity to test them in competition.

Plan a long warm-up and warm-down before and after the competition. The fans, officials, and rival teams will enhance the competitive atmosphere and will assure that swimmers make a good effort.

Preparing for the Regular Season Exception

What makes a regular season meet more important? A traditional team rival or the need to swim fast enough to meet the qualifying standards for the championship meet would be two good reasons. Sometimes an invitational meet will attract high quality competition to make it somewhat special.

    A SPECIAL MEET!

The Canada Cup meet, in Vancouver, BC, is a special meet for Tacoma Swim Club. Some of the best swimmers in the world attend this meet, including last year's national swim teams from Australia, China, Sweden, Italy, and the United States. Although we travel just 185 miles to compete in the Canada Cup, the fact that it occurs in a foreign country gives the meet an added significance.

Your swimmers' needs will vary in the preparation for any meet. Some athletes may want to swim fast but will not want to taper and rest to do it. Others may want to hold their conditioning level through the meet.

One or two mornings off from training during the week of a special meet is acceptable. Swimmers should avoid intense anaerobic training for a few days prior to the meet, and they should maintain or intensify race-pace, speed, and stroke focus. Most of the other swimming should be aerobic, which should help each swimmer race well in the competition without losing any training effect.

Preparing for the Championship Meet

You've directed your entire season toward success at this meet. Follow your season training plan up to the time period that you have designated for peak preparation, a process some coaches call "tapering." I prefer to call it peak preparation, because it minimizes the taper mentality that emphasizes only rest. Prepare swimmers for some very specific training at this time, focusing on every technical aspect, the most important ones being starts, turns, finishes, distance per stroke, stroke tempo, and race strategies.

One of the arts in coaching is the delicate balance between tapering and full training. Tapering too long can produce great speed but can leave the swimmer short of being able to sustain that speed over the complete race distance. Conversely, tapering for too short a time can leave swimmers flat and without the speed they need to be successful.

The Peak Preparation Period

Some believe the most important aspect of coaching is determining the length and intensity of the taper for each swimmer. Your self-confidence and your swimmers' confidence in your taper are vital for success. The peak preparation period should be long enough to permit the flexibility needed to adjust the taper's length and the intensity of its swimming.

As a coach of male swimmers, I planned my taper to last about 3 weeks in the short course high school program with a short championship meet. A few swimmers always tapered longer than others, so I adjusted for each individual from a general plan of 3 weeks.

Consider all of the following factors before you decide on the length of your taper or peak preparation, because these will effect the length of taper for each swimmer. Remember that you need flexibility to meet the swimmer's individual needs.

1. Male or female
2. Sprinter or distance swimmer
3. The swimmer's muscle mass
4. The length and type of championship meet
5. The swimmer's history
6. A short course or long course championship
7. The apparent effect of the season's training
8. The swimmer's age

Male or Female

Taper male swimmers longer than females in most situations, because men take longer to recover from intense training. If my peak preparation is going to be over a 3-week period for male swimmers, then I would shorten this to 2 weeks for most women swimmers.

Sprint or Distance Swimmer

Sprint swimmers usually taper best over a longer time period than that provided for distance swimmers.

For your distance swimmers, maintain intensive training and adequate aerobic endurance training closer to the championship meet. I would normally shorten the taper period for distance swimmers by at least 1 week or more when compared to sprinters.

The middle distance swimmers, those who compete primarily at the 200 and 400/500 events, would fall between the sprint and distance swimmers in the taper length.

Swimmer's Muscle Mass

Men generally need a longer taper than women, because of their muscle mass. This is also true within each sex; heavy muscled men usually need to taper more than those with less muscle density, and the more densely muscled women will usually need more rest or a longer taper than those with less density.

Length and Type of Championship Meet

A high school state championship meet is normally a 1- or 2-day meet. When it is 2 days, the prelims are usually one day and the finals the next. A U.S. swimming national championship meet is currently over 5 days, and the Olympic Trials are usually 6 days or more. Preparing for a short 1- to 2-day meet can sometimes take a longer taper than getting ready for a long 5- to 6-day meet.

History of the Swimmer

Know your swimmers and keep records of what works best for each individual. I have had swimmers who tapered best over a very long peak preparation of at least 5 weeks.

 HE TAPERED LONG FOR HIS SUCCESS

Bob Jackson, an NCAA Division II, collegiate All-America nose guard on the University of Puget Sound football team, was also an All-America breaststroke swimmer. He won the national long course 100-m breaststroke title in U.S. swimming while competing for Tacoma Swim Club.

I learned about his taper from his college coach and my good friend, Don Duncan. Bob was a heavy-muscled sprinter, so I tapered him 5 or 6 weeks, and he would come down to extremely low yardage on the final days.

Bob loved to taper long, and he never failed to produce his best swimming times after a long taper.

I have also had swimmers that needed to train very close to the meet—a few days, up to about 10. Normally, I would consider a 10-day taper to be on the short end of taper periods. In the long course season, 10-day tapers have worked well with my male distance swimmers and most of my females. Some female swimmers find 7-day tapers successful for the long course season.

Anything shorter than 7 days is cutting it close, but it may be necessary for swimmers who are low in self-confidence. Although you really need to be tapering these swimmers longer, you also need to build their confidence by giving them enough easy swimming that they believe that they are still working.

Short Course or Long Course

Long course events require more swimming than those of short course; each 100-m event is almost 30 ft longer than a 100-yd event.

The difference in swimming a 100-m event in long course is not just the additional distance when compared to a 100-yd race but also that a long course 100 m requires only one turn, while the short course 100 yd requires three. This means that you are not swimming when you turn and push off the wall. I calculate that a short course 100-yd event is about 67% swimming, when you subtract the nonswimming portions during the dive and three turns, whereas a long course 100-m event is about 83% swimming minus the dive and one turn.

In other words, the short course event results in 67 yd of actual swimming in a 100-yd event and 91 yd of actual swimming in a 100-m event. Given these differences, the long course taper cannot usually be quite as long.

Apparent Effect of the Season's Training

If an athlete is swimming very slow as you near the taper, then it may be necessary to taper the swimmer longer or more drastically. Swimmers will adapt to the stress placed upon them in training to different degrees. Your evaluation of a swimmer's need for additional rest may be critical for success at the championship meet.

MORE REST, NOT MORE WORK

Every coach has stories of swimmers who needed more rest, even bed rest, to return to peak form. Kaye Hall swam below expectations in the 100-m backstroke leg of the 400-m medley relay in the 1968 Olympic Games. The team was in third place after her backstroke leg.

Kaye then had 7 days before her individual race in the 100-m backstroke. The Olympic coach, Sherm Chavoor, allowed me to prepare her over those days. I had her swim easy, for a very short time each day and had her do drill work only. She also did some very short speed work but no race-pace or anaerobic swims. She went to the pool once a day and rested during the extra time provided, much of it bed rest.

At the end of her light training and rest, Kaye won the 100-m backstroke, the gold medal, and set the world record, swimming 1.5 s faster than her medley relay swim 1 week earlier. That one extra week of rest made the difference.

Swimmer's Age

Taper older swimmers longer than younger ones. Mature men and women need a longer taper than high school swimmers, and high school swimmers can taper longer than younger swimmers.

Prepuberty age-group swimmers don't respond in the same manner as older swimmers to the normal taper process. Leading up to the competition, these young athletes should swim fast in practice, and have very short rest periods, if any. Young age-group swimmers may respond psychologically in a peak preparation period, but don't expect a major physiological adjustment to their taper; for one thing, they have less muscle mass, and for another, they don't get as tired as mature swimmers during training.

Intensity of Training in the Taper

Control the intensity according to those same factors that you considered to determine the length of the taper. You must individualize your training schedule to a high degree at this stage of the season. I have had as many as eight different taper workout groups preparing for a state high school championship. In my final preparation, the fewest number of groups I've had has been three. Every swimmer must believe that the taper is designed for him or her.

COACH CONVENIENCE VERSUS SWIMMER PREPARATION

Conducting several different taper groups requires more time and planning from the coach. When I had many taper groups, I needed an additional hour of planning time each day. I also needed more time to communicate to my assistant coach and to my student managers the details of the plan and how they fit into it.

Organization was the key. Every assistant and swimmer knew what had to be timed and when it would happen. I always staggered the timed swims so that every athlete received individual coaching attention at some point in the session.

The successful results of this special attention to my swimmers' distinct tapers made any required extra coaching time more than worth the effort.

There *is* intensity training during the taper. Athletes must continue to know the feeling that comes from swimming fast; they just don't do as much of it, and what amount they do is highly specific to their events. You should reduce the swimmers' total yardage but have them maintain about an 80% effort on enough swims to hold their aerobic capacity through the taper.

The Three Rs

Coach Dave Haller, former Olympic coach of Great Britain and Hong Kong, spoke to my team just before our summer regional championship a few years ago. He stated that peak performance through a taper is very simple *if* the work has been done during the season's training. Keep it simple. Peak performance is made up of the three Rs: rest, relax, and rehearse.

Rest Rest is a patterned behavior, built on regular habits. If the swimmer is exceptionally tired, then more and more bed rest is essential. The swimmer must take care at the competition to maintain regular habits. It would be foolish for any swimmer to throw away months of intense training by losing focus close to the competition. This is no time for late nights or any other nonproductive behaviors.

Relax Swimmers should rest in a relaxed manner. They should put their minds at ease and not think of the competition. Stretching and loosening exercises help swimmers relax, as does playing games to get their minds free and easy.

Rehearse Swimmers need to establish specific patterns of behavior by getting up, entering the water, eating, and allowing for rest at certain times and then sticking with these patterns. Swimmers should mentally rehearse the start and the entire swim, visualizing themselves swimming fast yet easy. They should see themselves building their race, focusing on good turns, and having a strong finish. Rehearse the crowd conditions and whatever else may be a factor in the competition.

A THOUSAND TIMES IN YOUR MIND

My son, Dick, won the state championship in the 200 and 500 free events in his senior year of high school. Each of his swims were national high school records. He defeated a rival who held the state records for these events and had been the previous state champion for several years. His 200 national record broke Mark Spitz's national high school record.

After the meet, a reporter asked him if he was surprised by his wins and record times. He answered, "I was not surprised because I had swum those races a thousand times in my mind."

Peak Performance

I gave the following instructions in a handout to the Tacoma Swim Club going into the peak preparation period prior to the region championship.

"The championship meet has been the driving force of our training efforts throughout this winter season. Each of our goals would ideally be attained in our championship meet swims. Championship meet time is fast approaching. What can we now do to enable each of us to swim at our best in Beaverton or beyond?

"Training for the most part is over. We did or didn't do the necessary work by this time in our training. Our endurance training will be maintenance work only from now on. Specific race-pace swims to get sustained speed for our events will be the focus in our training."

Trip preparation

Most of our championship meets involve a trip away from home, the exception being age-group regionals. A swim meet away from home can be more tiring, because you will be sleeping in a different bed, making your food choices from a restaurant menu, and having other distractions. *Focus* through the complete championship. Many of us will have our best event(s) on the last day. *Rest*— plan to have a curfew for yourself. Get to bed each night as soon as possible after the competition. Plan a nap every day by getting back to your motel right after the preliminaries. Avoid getting trapped into a TV program that is beyond your *rest* time, and avoid any party atmosphere that depletes you before the competition is over.

Nutrition

A lot of your eating will be snacking at the meet and in the motel, but you will also be making food selections from a menu. Plan ahead and, ideally, you shouldn't change your eating habits drastically. All through the season, I have encouraged you to get eight servings of grains, four of fruit, three or four of vegetables, one or two of meat or fish, and two to four servings of nonfat or low fat dairy products each day. If you plan ahead, you can maintain this through the meet. Balance among the food groups will keep your glycogen levels adequate through the meet. When you are doing less training, some of you will have to take small servings to avoid gaining weight. Plan to bring healthy snacks only. *Hydrate*—bring your water jugs to the meet. Keep them full and drink water or a diluted sports drink frequently.

Mental rehearsal

The *mental* part of competing is most important. *Focus* on what you plan to do. If you are mentally tough all the way through each event, you will achieve good results. Every race-pace swim in training and at the meet must be visualized as part of your swim. Count strokes for stroke efficiency, both in training and in the warm-up at the meet. See yourself swimming the event. Visualize a perfect start, a super breakout stroke to capture the momentum of the dive, and an easy but fast swim with your planned breathing pattern. Focus on the wall and

the turn as you approach each wall. Build your speed into each wall, swimming strongly to it, and see yourself turning fast. Kick and break off the wall, again capturing the speed from the momentum of the push-off. See yourself getting stronger and building your speed in the second half of the race. Visualize yourself at your fastest and strongest on the final portion of the race. See yourself keeping your face in the water and concentrating on the final wall through the touch pad from the back flags to the finish. (Backstroke and breaststroke swimmers maintain your normal stroke and breathing, but build through the finish.)

Stay positive and tough. Cheering for your teammates is very important. When we cheer together and recognize the great performances, we give ourselves the best chance to be successful. MENTAL GIANTS or mental midgets? The choice is with each of us. Let's *go for it!*

Final preparation is sometimes called taper, but I prefer *peak preparation*

We are going into something special in peak preparation. Taper may indicate that we are coming away from something, usually hard training. Peak preparation requires some intense swimming. We need some of the most race-specific swims of the season at this time, and they don't always come easily. You won't be great every day during this period of time. Your body will be adapting, so just be sure that your mind is adapting too by being positive. The objective is to be great on race day.

The extra rest that you may be able to get in these final weeks will benefit you, so you must plan on nap time on weekends and avoid late nights from now on, including weekends. Talk to the coach if you have any questions or concerns.

Preparing the Relay Teams

Relays make swimming more of a team sport. Some athletes surpass their best times only when swimming relays, and some swimmers will always produce relay times that are at least as good as their individual race times. And naturally, there are some swimmers who will produce personal-best swims only in individual events. Because of these many possibilities, you need to know your swimmers and what to expect from them in relay swims.

Relays are exciting events, and it is not unusual to have the lead change several times during the race. High school swim meets begin and end with relays. They start with a 200-yd medley relay and end with a 400-yd free relay. At about midmeet, there is also a 200-yd free relay. The U.S. swimming national championship meets have three relay events, the 400 and 800 free relays and the 400 medley relay. These relays will be measured in meters in the long course championship and in yards in the short course.

Instructions to the Relay

I love coaching relays, because they bring a team together and draw a lot of fan focus. I instruct my relay team members on the importance of the event; if it is the first, I want them to think about getting our entire team hyped on their initial success.

I talk about team pride to our relay members. I tell them that it takes four swimmers to win a relay. I also tell them what I expect from them in order to win the relay event. Each swimmer must contribute his or her best in order for the final one to be in a position that will make winning possible.

I talk about our relay team tradition, about what a great one we've had both at Wilson High School and on Tacoma Swim Club. Remind swimmers to talk to each other on the blocks. The last swimmer must encourage the other three, while the first must inspire the others by his or her swim and by verbally encouraging the other relay members.

Position on the Relays

Position relay members according to the strengths of the swimmers and the distance of the relay event. The medley relay consists of four athletes who each swim a different stroke in the following order: backstroke, breaststroke, butterfly, and freestyle. The freestyle relay consists of four athletes who each swim the freestyle.

Medley Relays

You will usually go with your best swimmer in each of the four different strokes if they are available. Sometimes it is necessary to hold one or more of your best stroke swimmers out of the medley relay in order to have them available for a free relay later in the meet. In high school and college swimming, the medley relay is usually the first event. In the short 200 medley relay, each swimmer swims a 50 segment. In very short relays, I believe in getting out in front, because it takes a very strong swimmer to come from behind in a short relay.

Go for a very fast backstroke and breaststroke legs on a 200 medley relay. When the relay is out front and has some open water, the butterfly and/or the freestyle legs can be slightly weaker, because when out front, the final legs will have smoother and faster water to swim in. This is a good position, psychologically, for your weaker swimmers to be in to perform at their very best.

AN IMPORTANT EVENT

My Wilson High School teams always tried to win the 200-yd medley relay in the state championship meet, because it was the first event and provided a big mental boost to start the meet if they won.

I would always place strong back and breaststroke swimmers in the front two positions. I often held my best flyer and/or my best freestyle swimmer for the free relay. Year after year, our number two flyer or an even weaker freestyle swimmer would turn in a super swim to win the 200-yd medley relay.

Because it is longer, the 400 medley relay provides time for a good inside swimmer to bring this event from behind. I do not always emphasize getting out front with the first swimmers in this event, but I prefer using at least my best swimmers in the backstroke, breaststroke, and butterfly legs. You can get by with a weaker freestyle leg when you are strong in the first three.

Freestyle Relays

You have more options for the relay order in freestyle relays, because each swimmer swims the freestyle stroke. You must decide which order is best for different situations. Your options would include swimming 1, 2, 3, 4, which would be the fastest swimmer to the slowest. The more traditional order of relay swimmers is either 1 or 2 in the first position, 4 in the second, 3 in the third, and

1 or 2 in the anchor leg. You might use several other options depending on a number of other considerations. For example, if one swimmer came off of a preceding event, you might place her or him in a different relay position than you would have otherwise.

In the 200 free relay, which is short, I like my swimmers to get out front, if possible, for the fastest and smoothest water. Also, other teams must swim in your wake. I like a 1, 2, 3, 4 order in this relay.

In the 400 free relay, I like to use a little more variety in the order. I use a 1, 4, 3, 2 or a 2, 4, 3, 1 most frequently. I will also use a 1, 2, 3, 4 order in this relay for some of the same reasons that I would in the 200 free relay.

When we have a less than average chance to win a 400 relay, I like a 1, 2, 3, 4 order that attempts to break the other relay teams' will to win. If you get out front by as big a margin as possible, it makes it look extremely difficult to catch up. You can also pump up your anchor swimmer to make the swim of his or her life in this situation.

The 800 free relay is another story, because it is long enough for each swimmer to come from behind during each 200 leg. Consequently, I may use any relay order to best fit the situation.

I prefer an experienced and very strong anchor swimmer in the 800. An experienced fourth athlete will swim the full 200 strong and in control, which is very important when the swimmer dives in behind another relay. He or she must "reel in" the swimmer in front and not overswim the first part of the 200 trying to overtake the leading swimmer too quickly. Also, when the anchor swimmer is ahead and must hold off a very fast swimmer from the team behind, he or she must not overswim the first part of the relay.

 A MEMORABLE RELAY

Tacoma Swim Club's 800-m free relay team was swimming in the next to last heat in the finals of the 1974 U.S. Swimming National Long Course Championship meet. On that relay were two experienced college swimmers and two younger high school swimmers.

Our team got out fast and stayed out front to win that heat. We were surprised when we won the heat, especially when it was announced that we had broken the American club record for the event. The record belonged to us for less than 15 min, before it was broken again in the final relay heat. We finished a very good third in the event.

It was a relay to remember for my wife and myself not so much for the brief American club record but more for the makeup of the team. The names of the swimmers were Hannula, Hannula, Hannula, and Smith. Our sons, Dan, Dave, and Dick, had teamed up with Mark Smith at that championship.

Summary

Preparing for meets requires planning, and it is not the same procedure for every meet. The following points need to be considered:

1. Your major preparation should be for your championship meet.
2. All meets must contribute to preparation for the championship.
3. There are several types of inseason meets, and some may be more important than others.
4. The length of your peak preparation or taper will depend on a number of factors:
   - Male longer than female
   - Sprinters longer than distance
   - Heavy-muscle longer than slight or average
   - A short championship meet longer than a long championship meet
   - A swimmer's individual history
   - A short course meet longer than a long course meet
   - Highly trained and stressed swimmers longer
   - Older longer than younger

5. Individualize your workouts in the taper.
6. Remember the 3Rs: rest, relax, and rehearse.
7. Relays are a special focus in any meet.
8. Consider several factors when determining the order of your relay swimmers.

Chapter 13

Handling Meet Situations

Coach but don't overcoach; do most of it in the practice sessions and permit your athletes to test themselves in competition.

I keep my instructions at the competition short and to the point, because swimmers can only focus on a limited number of points when competing. I believe that a brief reminder regarding race control and sustained speed is a lot of coaching before an event.

In other words, avoid overcoaching at the competition, because too many instructions will overload and confuse your swimmers. Let them go out and compete, and then you can do the necessary coaching in your next practice sessions.

Be a Coach, Not a Critic

As a coach, be positive and try to avoid telling swimmers what they are doing wrong. You want to create a correct picture in their minds, so avoid negative images. Make your postevent evaluation brief and try to create a positive mental picture for the swimmer whenever possible. Say things like "Great race! I loved your finish!" or "Your stroke tempo was right on!" Any one of these may be enough coaching after an event in competition.

Avoid telling a swimmer that he or she destroyed the third turn or crashed on the back half of the race, because these are negative statements that create the wrong pictures in a swimmer's mind. They already know what they did wrong. Your job is to erase these pictures, not to perpetuate them. For instance, tell your swimmers to focus more on their buildup into the walls, and they will have stronger turns; tell them to be fast and easy with regular breathing cycles early in their race, and they will have a much stronger back half in their next swim. In short, be a coach and not a critic.

Keep It Simple

Brief and concise statements that are familiar work best. Tell swimmers what they have already heard from you during practice, because it will be comfortable to them and they can more easily process it.

⚬⚬⚬ A PRELIM TO FINAL ADJUSTMENT

At the U.S. Swimming Junior National Championship-West meet, one of my swimmers, Alycia Ladd, had a prelim swim in the 200-yd backstroke of 2:01.37. She was out fast in 57.78 and finished poorly in 1:03.59, for a 5.81 drop in the second 100.

After the event, I suggested that she ease off a little in the first 100 and then build the second to hold a sustained speed for the race in the final that night. Stroke tempo would be the key; she would go out with a slightly slower stroking tempo and come home with a faster one.

The final swim was a faster 2:00.17. She was out in 59.33 and got home in 1:00.84, for an excellent 1.51 drop in the second 100. By giving Alycia a positive image of good stroke tempo, I erased the negative picture of her previous finish.

Regular Season Meets Versus Major Meets

Dual and regular season meets prepare the team for the championship meets and are the purest form of training. During a practice session, it is impossible to completely duplicate the race-pace speed and competitive circumstances that exist in actual competition.

Correct your swimmers' racing mistakes during the dual meets and other regular season meets, because this is the time to learn how the swimmers race best. The dual meet season is your testing and learning period prior to the championship.

The Warm-Up

Teach the value of a good warm-up during the regular competitive season. Swimmers must know their best warm-up before the championship meet, so they will have more confidence when going into their most important meet of the season.

The warm-up has two phases. In the first, the primary concern is to loosen up and to feel comfortable in the water; the second is designed to prepare the swimmer's muscles, circulatory system, and nervous system for the major physical effort necessary in the event.

During the first part of the warm-up, athletes should swim a slow easy crawl. Emphasize a long streamlined glide off each wall. Swimmers must listen to their bodies and get a feel for the water, and they should avoid racing during this phase of warm-up.

Next, swimmers need to begin to include the best in basic technique. Include stroke drills and counting the number of strokes per length in this phase. Gradually increase the swimmers' intensity and heart rate by having them do some race-pace 50s or 100s. Having swimmers dive 25s or 12-1/2s may also be necessary for particular events. Finally, a brief warm-down should have the swimmer ready for competition.

The warm-up for competition is highly individualized. Swimmers must learn to understand their own bodies to maximize the chances for success from a good warm-up. After all, the purpose of a warm-up is preparing to swim fast, and the quality of a warm-up can make or break a good performance. Warm-ups are not the time to socialize and to cut corners, so swimmers must use them wisely.

After the warm-up, I advise my swimmers to dry off and to stay warm by wearing dry socks and shoes for the feet and sweatsuits for the rest of the body. In some outside conditions, parkas and gloves may be necessary.

If the main warm-up was concluded a long time before the swim, it may be necessary to loosen up again briefly prior to the competition. Swimmers should evaluate whether they need to return to a water warm-up prior to the swim. If the time period is less than 45 min or so, swimmers can decide if moving and stretching is enough preparation or if they need to return briefly to the water. When the waiting time is over 1 hour, I will usually advise a brief return to the water to loosen up.

The Warm-Down

Have your swimmers take the time to warm down sufficiently after their events. Just after their event, they should do some easy swimming in the main pool and then some in the diving or warm-up pool.

Swimming down in this manner will disperse lactic acid that has accumulated in the muscles after racing. Swimmers who warm down will have a much better chance to be successful in the meet's next race.

Home Versus Away

Training is usually reduced on the day you travel to a meet, because of the added time needed to travel. If the meet is during regular season, then you should attempt to schedule enough pool time to keep your swimmers aerobically fit.

Swimmers traveling by van or automobile will need to stretch out and walk around during stops. For longer trips, I recommend a stop at least every hour.

Riding in a van or automobile provides swimmers with additional rest. Sitting may be uncomfortable, but it does conserve energy, which is an important factor in each swimmer's favor at the competition.

AN EARLY COACHING EXPERIENCE

One year we travelled by automobiles for 2-1/2 days on a trip to California. Over that time we drove about 20 hr, and we slept out on the ground each night. The only swim we took on the trip was a recreational one in a fresh water lake. Basically, the swimmers were locked up in a car for more than 2 days, resulting in a "forced rest." We had one night's rest in a motel before starting a major 3-day meet.

The results were excellent; most everyone swam personal-best-ever times in their events. The forced rest seemed to be the best explanation for our success.

A Time Zone Change

Air travel often requires a change in time zones, so ask swimmers to begin adapting to the time zone change prior to departure. Within the continental United States, your time zone change may be 1, 2, or 3 hr.

If it is a 1-hr time change, swimmers should go to bed and arise 1 hr earlier or later depending on the direction traveled. If it is a 2- or 3-hr change, gradually alter the bedtime hours over the course of a week. I also adjust our practice schedule so that it is as close as possible to the same time schedule of the competition in the different time zone.

When competing in the same time zone, I am comfortable traveling up to the day before the meet, but when a change of zone is required, I prefer traveling a minimum of 1 day earlier than the day before for each hour of time zone change.

If we could not afford to travel several days early, then I would convince my swimmers to adjust to the new time zone prior to departure for the best results. Nine times out of ten, believing makes the adjustment work.

The Away Environment

Dual meet competition at a traditional rival's pool requires some special coaching. Visualizing the environment, including the spectator involvement, can help prepare the team.

Before we depart for a meet, I want my swimmers prepared for the home team's band, their cheerleaders, and their crowd's enthusiasm. Stories of past swim meets can do much to have your team ready for the unexpected.

EXPECT THE UNEXPECTED

In my first year at Wilson High School, we swam an away meet at a 20-yd pool in Olympia. It was the first dual meet of the season that Wilson had lost, and we only lost two dual meets in 25 years. I considered it a disaster because I had not prepared our team for a tough meet in a hostile environment and in a shorter pool. I learned from this experience.

Another major rival was Don Fairbairn at Port Angeles High School. He was the son of my own high school coach and a tough competitor. The coaching staff always prepared the swimmers for Port Angeles, because we knew Don would always have the fans, press, and officials at fever pitch for our meet.

I would explain to our swimmers to be prepared for some "hometown" decisions in officiating. This was before automatic timing machines were in use. Because we knew that we had to clearly win our races, we were able to hold our composure for questionable judging decisions. We had some memorable swim meets in Port Angeles, and I always enjoyed their competition.

The ability of the swimmers to keep their heads and to maintain focus will make the difference between winning and losing. Nothing quiets hostile fans quicker than swimming fast and competing tough.

You should always expect the unexpected. You are going to lose some close races. However, if you keep the team focused, you will all be victorious.

We rehearse as many of the meet conditions as possible before we travel to an away meet. Pictures of the pool or previous videotapes of meets in the pool will help to prepare swimmers.

STATE MEETS IN THE UNIVERSITY OF WASHINGTON POOL

When I coached Wilson High School, the state meets used to be held in the University of Washington pool. The U of W pool was built in the 1930s and had tile turning lines that were extremely narrow, half the width of today's standard lines. It wasn't a turning T but rather just a line on the bottom and end walls.

I had our shop teacher make a sheet metal copy of the U of W turning line. He painted it white with a black line the same size as that at the U of W. It hung from our pool gutter and covered our own turning T completely.

We practiced on those improvised turning lines for the final few weeks of our season. Consequently, we were always ready for the turning walls at the University of Washington.

Individual Readiness

I have stated frequently in this book that our team's physical readiness depended on the stage of the season. If you stick to your season plan, you will be physically prepared at the championship meet, with the possible exception of illness and injury.

Swimming is a technique-driven sport, and as a result, some swimmers may need to refocus on technique. An individual swimmer may need some stroke adjusting at a particular time in order to compete successfully, so be prepared to coach technique when necessary to help a swimmer improve. Refocusing on technique can help the swimmer maintain

self-confidence. I believe that you must tell swimmers what you expect from them in competition, because it provides direction and realistic expectations for them.

Personal Conduct

Swimmers must learn to be proud of their good efforts in competition as well as in practice. Whether they win or lose, swimmers should act with class. Congratulating opponents after a race should be a habit.

We played some very important and fun games at Wilson High School that effectively taught us better habits both in practice and competition.

Turkey Talk

Every Thanksgiving season, I would introduce our Wilson High School team to "turkey talk." We used a number of descriptive terms to establish the basic premise that turkeys were dumb birds. Swimmers would lose points on their season chart for any "turkey" acts during the season.

One or more of the following would qualify a swimmer for the rank of turkey: a swimmer who neither warms up nor warms down; a swimmer who loses the count of the number of lengths completed in a race; a swimmer who practices slow turns; a swimmer who false starts out of an event; a swimmer who coughs, cries, moans, or grimaces at the end of a race, or sprints the last 15 yd of a longer race after taking a bath through the preceding sections; anyone who talks a lot and walks a lot in practice or in premeet warm-up; and, finally, anyone who stops a lot, especially in midpool. I always say that turkeys gather in flocks, and that if one turkey stops, all the others will stop to find out why.

Swimming Fast or Making Excuses

"Punker," the second name game we played, applied more closely to competitive situations than even the turkey game. I tried to encourage individual responsibility through the punker game by subtracting points from anyone who earned punker status.

One of our posters read "A punker always has a good excuse." I would list the number of good excuses that I had heard

in my coaching career. It would usually total two, one I heard maybe 20 years earlier, and another only 5 years ago. The idea of the game was to give swimmers little opportunity to make excuses for a low effort or a poor performance. I wanted them to make their own choices and to take responsibility for the consequences of their actions.

Name games like turkey and punker teach swimmers some good competitive habits and how to handle adversities like defeat or a poor swim.

Strategic Decisions

You will establish most of your decisions on who will swim each event before the meet. Yet, there are always some swimmers who are probable in a particular event. In dual meets, this flexibility is possible, but in championship meets, you can't usually make changes. An upset in one event and a score differential may necessitate a lineup change in midmeet in a dual meet.

Before the meet, prepare your team for the possibility of lineup changes. For example, you might say that Jim will swim the 200 free and the 100 butterfly, unless the score indicates otherwise after the first relay. Jim

may swim the 200 individual medley or the 100 free if necessary. Such foresight on the coach's part will prepare Jim and his teammates for this possibility.

Explain the reasons for your lineup choices when you announce them to your team, because they need to understand them in order to feel a part of the decision. Sometimes they need to have direct input into their event selection, particularly when the championship meet rolls around.

MORE THAN ONE WINNER

I always held a meeting with each swimmer to pick the events that she or he would swim at the championship meet. I always sought to balance team need with individual choice.

In our 1970 state high school championship, I had my four best freestylers select the 200 free as one of their best events. I then pointed out to each of them the fact that we now had our four best swimmers in the same event. They all looked me in the eye and said, "I can win, coach." Because the outcome of the meet was not in doubt, I said to each of them, "Go for it."

The event was loaded with the best talent in the state. Our four boys went a very close 1, 2, 3, and 4 in the event, all at personal-best times. They were all winners on that day and I have always respected them for the courage of their convictions.

Meet and Postmeet Concerns

There are both individual and team concerns at and after the meet that you must be prepared to deal with at all times.

Premeet Talks

In a regular season meet, I talk to my swimmers about team and individual pride. I tell them that they can always race tough, even if they can't race fast. I let them know that I expect an honest effort in each of their races, without any special rest or taper. Usually, you do not need to do more than this.

For the regular season exception, I talk in much the same way, but I tell them I expect them to reach a little deeper for this special occasion. If we have a morning or two off from training, I will remind them of it and will suggest that they should be better than usual.

I also ask them to focus on sustained speed. All meets are a dress rehearsal for the championship, and we will be our best when we can hold our speed through the middle and the finish of our races. I may ask them for their predictions of their race times and split times, because this helps maintain focus.

I discussed the championship meet talk already in chapter 12, under peak preparation. Personal pride, team pride, and sustained speed would continue to be points of emphasis throughout the championship meet.

Running Score

Have one of your managers keep a running score throughout the meet to assure that no clerical error occurs. Any discrepancy must be reported to the coach immediately.

Split Times

After every event, you must record your swimmers' split times. Stroke counts and stroke rates would also be valuable information for each event, and we do this whenever possible. Each swimmer should go over the split times to better prepare for the next race.

Postmeet Team Meeting

When you win, the postmeet team meeting should be held the next day, because it will likely be more effective after the natural high of winning abates. On the other hand, when you lose, you should have your team meeting right after competing. Don't let the team dwell on a loss; they need their coach at this time to focus on the bright spots and on the future.

THE SECOND DUAL MEET LOSS

Wilson High School lost its second dual meet in my last year of coaching, 24 years after the first loss. I talked to the team immediately after the meet and told them that I was proud of them and nothing had changed. I let them know that we were on schedule and headed for a great state championship. It was the right timing given the situation.

Summary

When coaching meets, you must adhere to some basic principles, such as the following:

1. Avoid overcoaching.
2. Focus on a few specific points.
3. Coach in a positive way.
4. Use brief and concise statements because they work best.
5. Correct mistakes during the regular or dual meet season.
6. Teach an effective warm-up to your swimmers.
7. Warm-ups must be individualized.
8. Warm down sufficiently after racing.
9. Adjust for time zone changes prior to departure.
10. Prepare for the away meet environment.
11. Tell your swimmers what you expect from them.
12. Teach proper personal conduct.
13. Give your swimmers some say in their event selection.
14. Be there for your team when they lose.

Part V

Coaching Evaluation

Chapter 14

Evaluating Swimmers' Performances

You should constantly evaluate your swimmers and your own coaching. I want to know how my swimmers are adapting to my training program. I may evaluate the results of our endurance training weekly or over a period of several weeks. However, I evaluate each swimmer's progress in stroke technique daily.

Always base your evaluations on the swimmers' individual abilities and starting point. Don't judge the average swimmer based on the performance of the best one.

 THE LAST CAN BE FIRST

In practice, my most glowing evaluation will often go to my slowest swimmer. When one of our lowest level swimmers does his or her best set of repeat swims in practice, I focus the spotlight on that person, because such recognition

for practice effort always inspires our entire team, especially when it comes to one of the lower level swimmers.

I base my preseason evaluation on first, the swimmer's attendance, and second, his or her work habits, both of which are necessary early steps for helping the swimmer adapt both physically and mentally to the training.

Practices

It is the will to prepare to win that counts. Through success in practice, swimmers attain mental toughness and confidence. I think of each practice session as an opportunity for swimmers to invest in their own success; they will get out of their competitions only what they put in during the practices. Practices offer the coach the opportunity to establish baseline performance levels for swimmers and then the chance to evaluate their progress.

Observations

Observe your swimmers in practice and require good technique from them even when they are tired from training. Continue to teach basic skills in all practice sessions, watching for fast turns, streamlined push-offs, and distance per stroke. Swimmers doing great things and doing them right in practice will be dynamite in competition.

I watch my swimmers from as many angles as possible during practice—from the side of the pool, at the end of the lane (the swimmer both coming and going), overhead, and underwater. Find a high overhead view for an excellent position to evaluate technique.

Whenever possible, you should also observe your swimmers underwater. Take advantage of underwater observation windows when they are available, or go into the water with a face mask, if that is the only thing available. I used a face mask one workout a week in most of my high school coaching.

Look at your swimmers from an upside-down viewpoint by lowering your head and looking under your armpit. If you lean over slightly with your back to the pool, you will see more and enhance your understanding of how the water flows off the swimmer's arms and around the body. Strange as this sounds, I guarantee that it works.

Recognize when your swimmers are "stale" from training by observing their performance levels. When practice has deteriorated to the point that most team members have lost their enthusiasm, it is time to make a change in your coaching approach. One thing to do is introduce some fun into the training by lightening up your approach and creating some excitement through change. Take a day off from training if necessary. Training results will soon improve again when you do this.

Record Keeping

Keep a record of daily attendance, because success in competition usually correlates with good attendance. Often, attendance records can help explain the success or failure of any particular swimmer. Individual conferences with a swimmer will benefit from keeping a record of that swimmer's attendance. A written attendance record can jolt a swimmer into reality because swimmers often don't realize that a lack of attendance can be at the root of a performance problem.

I make a written log of all my training sessions, and these are based on my season plan, as I outlined it in chapter 5. This log gives me an accurate record of exactly what each swimmer did in training day by day.

Record your swimmers' practice times every day whenever appropriate. For each main set, swimmers report their times from the pace clocks at the ends or sides of the pool. Swimmers must learn how to do this accurately. Occasionally, every swim is hand-timed. Recording the practice times motivates swimmers, and you will have a written record to refer to when necessary. You can measure in your written log both the intensity of the training and the swimmer's success in training.

I will also record the swimmer's heart rate in an occasional training set. The swimmers usually count their own heart rate, but I have also used a heart rate monitor for more accuracy. Heart rate monitors—many of the new ones coming on the market are easy to use and very accurate—measure intensity more accurately than other methods, and as a result you can determine which training sets are most effective. By monitoring heart rate, you can also tell when a swimmer is failing to adapt to particular training sets.

Both practice times and heart rates can indicate the degree of the swimmer's adaptation to training. If a swimmer is failing to adapt, you can take steps quickly to correct it.

Whenever possible, I like to record the stroke count per 50 in race-pace sets—the number of strokes the swimmer takes through 50 yd or 50 m. I also record stroke rate in race-pace sets to indicate the proper stroke tempo for each swimmer. I use a special stroke rate watch that gives me the number of strokes per minute.

I believe that weekly skin fold tests should also be recorded, because keeping such a record encourages swimmers to be aware of their nutrition sources and to be alerted when their body fat percentages are on the increase.

Event: _____   **Swimmer:** _____

Segments:	50	100	150	200	250	300	350	400
Split times:	____	____	____	____	____	____	____	____
Segments:	____	____	____	____	____	____	____	____
Stroke rate:	____	____	____	____	____	____	____	____
Number strokes:	____	____	____	____	____	____	____	____

Drop-off: 50 _____   50 _____   Total _____
            100 _____   100 _____   Total _____
            200 _____   200 _____   Total _____

Event: _____   **Swimmer:** _____

Segments:	50	100	150	200	250	300	350	400
Split times:	____	____	____	____	____	____	____	____
Segments:	____	____	____	____	____	____	____	____
Stroke rate:	____	____	____	____	____	____	____	____
Number strokes:	____	____	____	____	____	____	____	____

Drop-off: 50 _____   50 _____   Total _____
            100 _____   100 _____   Total _____
            200 _____   200 _____   Total _____

Figure 14.1   A sample record form for events over distances of 100 to 400 yards or meters a) blank and b) with data.

Meets

As I stated previously, I consider meets the purest form of training. Competition results should not be measured in individual wins or losses. Meets are a learning experience, and it is up to you as the coach to assure that they are positive.

Observations

Observe your swimmers to determine the weaknesses to improve and the strengths to praise. Record segments of the race that will enable the swimmer to train and race better in the future.

Watch each of your swimmers during the competition. I look for aggressiveness, stroke count, stroke rate, race pace, race tactics, breathing patterns, stroke technique, the start, turn, and finish skills, and sustained speed.

Aggressiveness, race tactics, breathing patterns, stroke technique, and start, turn, and finish skills are somewhat subjective to measure and require more coaching art, because you have to determine what and how much to throw at your swimmers.

Stroke count, stroke rate, split times, and sustained speed can and must all be measured objectively for each swim. You can train managers and assistant coaches to do this job (see Figures 14.1 and 14.2).

I can see more and better when I only observe the race, so I let my manager or assistant coach take split times. When I take split times, I miss too many technical aspects of

	Running Time	Segment 50s	Segment 100s	Segment 500/550s	Stroke Rate	Stroke Count
50						
100						
150						
200						
250						
300						
350						
400						
450						
500						
550						
600						
650						
700						
750						
800						
850						
900						
950						
1000						
1050						
1100						
1150						
1200						
1250						
1300						
1350						
1400						
1450						
1500						
1550						
1600						
1650						

Drop-off: (500)   250 _____   250 _____   Total _____

(800)   400 _____   400 _____   Total _____

Segment split times: (1500/1650)

500/550 _____   500/550 _____   500/550 _____

Figure 14.2   A sample record form for events from distances of 500 to 1650 yards or 800 to 1500 meters.

the race. My attention needs to be focused only on the swim itself. I also like to use my swimmers who are not competing in that event to take turns taking the splits, because it gives them some ownership in the process and makes them more aware of the value of such records.

In this way freed from record keeping, I can talk to swimmers about the technical aspects of their races throughout the competition, I can go over split times and help each swimmer evaluate the race, and I can encourage and attempt to motivate swimmers when necessary.

 OBSERVING FROM AFAR

Occasionally, I will remove myself from the pool deck in a training type of swim meet. For example, on its one side, the 50-m outdoor pool in Gresham, Oregon, has very high bleacher seating on the side of a hill. At this training meet, I sat on the last row of bleachers at midpool as high up as I could get. I was able to observe my swimmers and all of their racing weaknesses clearly. I made notes of our need to improve spe-

cific racing skills and conferred with each swimmer as necessary. We then worked in practice sessions to remedy these weaknesses.

You should only take this approach in specific situations, such as the type of meet described here. This pool had high observation points, and the meet did not require on-the-deck motivation.

Record Keeping

Record split times for every event. When possible, record the stroke rate and the stroke count for each segment of the event. These records will be invaluable for your swimmers and yourself in planning for future improvement.

Examples of record forms for specific distances appear in Figures 14.1 and 14.2. Make copies of these records and give them to each swimmer, because they provide critical information for you and the swimmer. Split times that include the running time, the segment times, and the drop-off for the event are a minimum requirement; I recommend recording stroke rate and stroke count whenever possible.

Summary

Evaluate your swimmers' performances both in practice and in competition. If you want change, then measure the results of both the practice sessions and the competition.

1. Practices reflect the will of your team to prepare to win.
2. Observe your swimmers in practice from as many different angles as possible.
3. Require great technique in practice if you want it in competition.
4. Record daily attendance at your practice sessions.
5. Make a written log of each training session throughout the season.
6. Record the practice times and the heart rate for each swimmer in the main sets.
7. At the competition, delegate the taking and recording of split times and other information to others; this will permit you to focus on all aspects of each race.
8. Make a written record of split times and other information to discuss with each swimmer.
9. Give copies of the meet records to each swimmer.

Chapter 15

Evaluating Your Program

Evaluate your program continuously, considering first whether you are still following your season plan. If you do this at least weekly throughout the season, you can determine if you need to make training adjustments in your season plan.

Of course, the major evaluation of your program must be made at the end of the season. Look at your program as soon as possible after the last championship meet, because that is the time when the results are most clear to you and your swimmers. Putting it aside until you are ready to deal with it may obscure some of the necessary details.

Make your evaluations as objectively as possible. You know when you have attained your goals and done the best that you were capable of.

 CONGRATULATIONS AND YOUR HEAD

We have won at least one state championship meet where I knew that we had not done our best over the season. The press and our boosters were most congratulatory over the fact that we had maintained our undefeated record and had won another consecutive championship meet.

However, I knew that we hadn't done our best, and my postmeet evaluation verified my feelings. We hadn't met the goals that we had set for ourselves. We had swum faster at the championship meet than our previous best, but not by much. From that evaluation, I made adjustments in planning for the next season, and it was a very successful one; we attained major drops again in our best times at the state championship meet. A critical look at your own performance can keep you hungry and in high anticipation for the approaching new season.

As the saying goes, "If you are satisfied, you are finished." A kick in the pants delivered by yourself to yourself can keep you aimed in the right direction—up.

Evaluating Personnel

At the start of the season, swimmers listed their goals, and now, at the end, it is time to sit down with each swimmer and come to some conclusions. Did they reach their goals? Why did or didn't they reach them? This is a good time to help each swimmer learn how to set goals. In general, young inexperienced swimmers are more prone to set goals that are too difficult to reach in the short run. They are often in the "dream" phase of the goal-setting process.

Lost time from illnesses or injuries can be analyzed objectively at this time, as well as a review of the training that each swimmer accomplished. Write a statement for the swimmers based on your own evaluation first, and share with them any positive input.

Next, have your swimmers give their own personal views, so you can learn from them. Swimmers may have perceptions that are not valid, but if they believe them, you need to know. I like to have my swimmers complete a questionnaire prepared by me (see Figure 15.1). This is a good way to draw out information from the swimmers, especially the younger, inexperienced ones.

A copy of this questionnaire should be given back to each swimmer at the start of the next season when you are in the goal-setting process. The swimmers' self-evaluation will help them to better focus on the elements of success in their next season, and it will help you to remind them where they need to improve.

When you evaluate personnel, you aren't considering replacements, unless you are able to recruit new swimmers (e.g., a college program might make a special effort to recruit a backstroker). High school and club programs are usually limited to the swimmers available to them, and this limitation is generally based on geography.

Finally, you need to determine whether you have the swimmers in their best events both in the stroke and the distance. Make decisions that will place swimmers in their most effective events for the coming season.

Evaluating Staff

I was a head high school coach without an assistant for about 12 years. This was also true when I first started as a club coach. If you are the only staff member in your coaching situation, then you have to evaluate what you did best and assign student managers to do what work they can do. This will give you more time to do your coaching, as it did me.

I always evaluated my managers, and I liked to do it informally after practice. They would report the results of timed swims and other parts of the practice for which they were responsible, and then we would talk about what went well and what we needed to do better. I was never critical of these volunteer managers, and I always praised their contributions to the success of our team. My wife and I took them out to dinner on one special night every season.

If you have assistant coaches, you need to evaluate their performances in order to get the best from each of them. Evaluate your assistant coaches the same way that you do yourself. Delegate to them those duties that they do best and retain those that you do best. The bottom line is for you to have quality time to coach.

Make sure that your staff members understand their responsibilities and duties, and encourage assistants to develop a plan that will carry out their duties more effectively.

I prefer talking to my assistants in a postseason meeting that is social as well as businesslike. A dinner or lunch meeting at my expense is an ideal setting. In a relaxed and comfortable setting, we can review the effectiveness of our collective coaching.

Questions for discussion should include these:

- What responsibilities do you feel confident in performing?
- What responsibilities do you feel the head coach must perform?
- What were the strengths of our staff?
- What were the weaknesses of our staff?

"Build for the future by looking back"

Name: _____

1. Which goals did you achieve that you set for yourself this past long course season?

2. Which goals did you not achieve that you set for yourself this past season?

3. Rate your effort in the following training areas this past season (Score 0 to 10 with 10 as the highest possible score):

(a) _____ Stretching	(m) _____ Race-pace sets
(b) _____ Tubing	(n) _____ Anaerobic high quality sets
(c) _____ Sled/bench	(o) _____ Power rack sets
(d) _____ Sit-ups/push-ups	(p) _____ Pulling sets
(e) _____ Attendance	(q) _____ Sculling
(f) _____ Maintaining goal focus	(r) _____ Drills
(g) _____ Positive mental attitude	(s) _____ Starts, turns, finishes
(h) _____ Regular season meet performance	(t) _____ Rest/sleep
(i) _____ Championship meet performance	(u) _____ Nutrition
(j) _____ Endurance one (A.T.) sets	(v) _____ Kicking sets
(k) _____ Aerobic endurance sets	(w) _____ Stroke count
(l) _____ Explosive speed sets	

4. What did you do best, based on your scores and other areas that you feel are important?

5. What could you have done better, based on your scores and other areas that you feel are important?

6. Rate the following areas according to their importance for you to become the best that you can be in swimming (Score 0 to 10 as before):

(a) _____ Mental approach to swimming	(f) _____ Hidden training (nutrition and rest)
(b) _____ Goal-setting	(g) _____ Handling adversity
(c) _____ Following coach's training	(h) _____ Self-discipline
(d) _____ Dryland training	(i) _____ Inner toughness
(e) _____ Swimming training	(j) _____ Stroke technique

Figure 15.1 A sample questionnaire given to swimmers at the end of a summer long course season.

- How was our communication? Did we always understand our daily, weekly, and season plans?
- What suggestions would you make to make our coaching better?

These questions will provide a basis for positive input from your staff and give you the opportunity to make suggestions to them. Take written notes of the meeting, and let your staff know that you value their input and that you intend to implement those suggestions that you mutually agree upon.

Replace a staff member only when absolutely necessary. When your respective philosophies conflict, you might need to make the decision to dismiss an assistant. Usually, however, I have to convince my lowly-paid assistant coaches to come back for another season, simply for the love of doing it.

ONE MORE YEAR

I had several great assistant coaches at Wilson High School and Tacoma Swim Club. At Wilson High School, Jim Boettcher was an art teacher who had a great eye for analyzing strokes and especially for seeing the components of successful dives. He was an excellent teacher and coach.

Each year I used all of my persuasive powers to get "one more year" out of him. I still consider myself lucky to have talked him into one more season no less than nine times.

I always was at my best when I had an assistant coach who wanted to be a head coach. This friendly working competition made us both better coaches, and our teams benefited from this type of relationship, because it wasn't adversarial. Many of my assistant coaches later headed their own programs. Dan Wolfrom has won several state championships at Foss High School in Tacoma, including both boys' and girls' in one year.

Evaluating Equipment

Evaluate the equipment that you are using at the end of each season. Are you using it most effectively? Do you need to make some changes in its use or perhaps in the equipment itself? Each year, there's new equipment on the market that you need to evaluate, because some of it may be a valuable addition to your program. I have added something new to our program every year. It keeps the program new and exciting to me and to the swimmers as well.

Evaluating Facilities

Regardless of the number of facilities available to you, you must use what you have in the most effective manner. Never limit your expectations for swimming success on the available facilities. Swimmers who have set world records have had to do the bulk of their training in pools as short as 50 ft. What you do and how you do it is more important than where you do your training.

The ideal training facility would have space for dryland training, long course and short course training, and an area for very short pool training (35-50 ft). I have never had all of these available in any one facility. Most often, you will have to evaluate how you can better organize the use of your facility to get the most from it.

Evaluating Your Own Performance

Judge your own performance as objectively as possible. Look at your season plan and evaluate it completely. (You should already have been making weekly evaluations throughout the season). Now is the time to determine if your results at the championship meets indicate that it was the best plan.

You need to think about how the season plan could have been improved. I have never had a season where I wanted to do the very same thing again. Some adjustments always need to be made. Something can always be done better.

Evaluate the confidence of your swimmers in you. Do they trust your recommendations and your judgment? Are you secure in your decisions? Are you consistent in your discipline and in treatment of your swimmers? You are the rock upon which your team is built. Were you that rock they needed at both the low and high points of the season?

Determine when and where you could have been better. Read and listen objectively to the evaluations of your swimmers and assistants. Act on their suggestions but avoid reacting. You have the opportunity to become a better coach by listening to your swimmers and assistants.

In addition to the questions already listed, consider scoring yourself on the following points when you evaluate yourself:

1. Your positive outlook
2. Your mental focus
3. Your communication with swimmers
4. Your communication with parents
5. Your use of your staff
6. Your consistency in teaching
7. Your ability to keep everything in perspective
8. Your ability to keep your program both challenging and fun

You can learn from your swimmers and your staff by asking them to evaluate you.

You can learn a lot from their questionnaires at the season's end. You can even go beyond this and ask them to rate you in many of the same areas on the questionnaire. I have done this, and you can always learn from their input.

 DEFLATING MY EGO

I have received more than a few jolts in my self-perception as a coach from questionnaires that I have given to my swimmers. In my experience, most of the questionnaire feedback has been positive and has reinforced the direction and methods of my coaching. However, I have had responses from swimmers who thought that I didn't like them. Nothing could have been further from the truth, and we worked it out satisfactorily after talking.

As a result of these misunderstandings, I have become more sensitive to the feelings of the young athletes that I coach. I have learned to recognize more of the misconceptions of my athletes and to make the necessary corrections before major problems erupt.

Evaluating Your Own Goals

Determine where you did and didn't meet your own goals. Were they too high or too low? Were they specific enough? Whatever your answers to such questions, always strive to measure your goals accurately.

Based on these evaluations, you can begin to set your goals for the next season.

Decisions Made From Your Evaluations

After your evaluations, make decisions that will have a positive effect on your program in the coming season. Don't wait to make these decisions; tackle them immediately after the end of the season.

 MORE SPEED WORK

After evaluating one of our team's long course season results, we determined that much of our success was the result of adding speed work every day. It was the only major change that we had made during the season, and our results had improved dramatically. I added daily speed work over very short distances to all of our subsequent seasons with excellent results.

No evaluation process in itself can make changes. You have to be willing to follow the guidelines that result from the evaluation process in order to better your program. In order to grow as a coach, you must be somewhat flexible when it comes to improving the program.

Correcting Problems

Sit down with your staff, the team, each swimmer individually, their parents, the administrators, or anyone else necessary in order to correct problems. Talk to them sometimes as a group and sometimes individually, one on one. Everyone wants to be and do better, and now is the time to agree on the best future plan of action.

The human side of any problem equation is the most challenging to correct. When everyone understands the situation clearly and works together to correct the problem, your next season has a much better chance for success.

Problems with equipment, facilities, and other items are easier to correct, because you can readily make decisions that are available to you usually without treading on human emotions. However, it still may be best to discuss changes, so that every team member understands the reasons for them.

Building Stronger for the Future

Once you've evaluated all aspects of your program and made your decisions regarding changes, it is time to enthusiastically anticipate the next season. Swimmers will have received their own self-evaluations back from you at the start of the new season, and this should make them more aware of the ingredients for success.

Sell your new season's program through your enthusiasm. Let everyone know the part they played in planning for the new season through their season-end questionnaires.

Summary

1. Your major program evaluation should come after the last championship meet.
2. Have your swimmers complete a prepared questionnaire at the end of the season.
3. Evaluate your assistant coaches' performance as well as your own.
4. Evaluate new equipment that may be needed, and determine the effectiveness of the old equipment.
5. Your chances for success do not depend on the facility available to you.
6. Correct those problems that have been identified.
7. Changes for the next season must be determined from your evaluation process.

Photo Credits

Index

About the Author

There are few awards or honors for swimming coaches that Dick Hannula doesn't hold. His impressive record at Wilson and Lincoln High Schools in Tacoma, Washington—414 wins, 29 losses, 1 tie—includes 323 consecutive meets without a loss, making him the winningest high school swimming coach in U.S. history. Dick also coaches the team at the Tacoma Swim Club, which he founded in 1955. His contribution to the sport of swimming was honored when he was inducted into the International Swimming Hall of Fame in 1987. He has received the Hall of Fame Award from the National Interscholastic Swimming Coaches' Association (NISCA) as well as the National Collegiate and Scholastic Swimming Trophy. The National High School Coaches' Association selected Dick as the National High School Swimming Coach of the Year in 1980.

Dick is one of swimming's most recognized authorities. He has served four terms as president of the American Swim Coaches' Association and has frequently held a seat on the ASCA board. He has served as chairman of the U.S. Swimming Technical Planning Committee and of the U.S. Swimming Technical Instruction Committee. In 1990, Dick served as Commissioner of Swimming for the Goodwill Games. He was the manager for the 1984 and 1988 U.S. Olympic teams. At the Pan Am Games, he has been both an assistant coach and the head manager. He has coached the U.S. National Team five times.

Dick has coached some of the best to greatness. His former students include 4 Olympic swimmers, including Kaye Hall;

three National Champions; and five winners in the World Student Games.

When Dick's not coaching, he's in high demand as a clinic speaker and instructor. A frequent author on swimming mechanics and coaching, Dick also writes a technical article for each issue of the NISCA magazine.

Dick Hannula and his wife, Sylvia, live in Tacoma, Washington. They have four children who have captured many swimming honors themselves, including a National Championship. Away from the pool, Dick enjoys fishing and foreign travel.

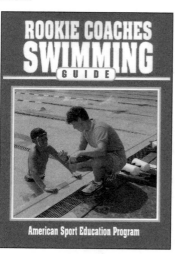

ADDITIONAL SWIMMING RESOURCES

The unique progression of skills in this book will help swimmers get started quickly, make steady progress, practice in performance contexts, and correct problems as they develop.

Second Edition •1996 • Paper • 160 pp
Item PTH00846 • ISBN 0-87322-846-4
$15.95 ($22.95 Canadian)

Swimming Instructor Guide Software

The *Instructor Guide Software* follows the same skill progressions as the participant's book and features warm-up and cool-down exercises, management and safety guidelines, 82 drills to fit various skill levels, rating charts for identifying students' skill levels, teaching cues to maximize learning, suggestions for identifying and correcting errors, and a complete test bank of written questions.

Windows Item PTH00638 • Macintosh Item PTH00639 • 1996 • 3-1/2" disk • FREE to course adopters

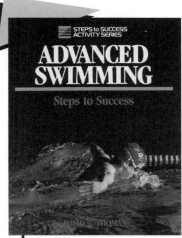

The second-level continuation of *Swimming: Steps to Success* features 18 steps designed to help swimmers review and improve the crawl and breast strokes, learn the new competitive back and butterfly strokes, and master competitive strokes and turns.

1990 • Paper • 168 pp • Item PTH00389
ISBN 0-88011-389-8 • $15.95 ($22.95 Canadian)

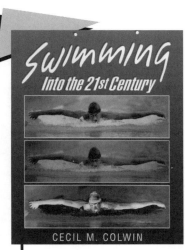

This book takes a comprehensive look at the evolution, science, and coaching application of competitive swimming. Packed with ground-breaking research and practical advice, the book presents a panoramic perspective of every phase of competitive swimming and looks at where it has been, where it is, and where it is going.

1992 • Paper • Item PCL00456
ISBN 0-87322-456-6 • $19.95 ($29.95 Canadian)

Special Book and Videotape Package

1/2" VHS *Diving My Way* video and *Ron O'Brien's Diving for Gold* book
Item MOBR0236
$39.95 ($59.95 Canadian)

Ron O'Brien's Diving for Gold emphasizes the basic skills needed for springboard and platform diving. More than 700 illustrations present the fundamentals of diving in the order the coach and diver should use them.

1992 • Paper • 200 pp • Item POBR0448 • ISBN 0-88011-448-7 • $19.95 ($27.95 Canadian)

Diving My Way is an excellent way to reinforce the information found in *Ron O'Brien's Diving for Gold*. Using slow-motion and stop-motion photography, the video highlights the latest techniques and concepts for a wide range of dives.

1/2" VHS • 1990 • Item MOBR0235 • $24.95 ($37.50 Canadian)

HUMAN KINETICS
The Premier Publisher for Sports & Fitness
P.O. Box 5076, Champaign, IL 61825-5076
www.humankinetics.com

To place your order, U.S. customers

Call 1-800-747-4457

Customers outside the U.S. place your order using the appropriate telephone number/address show in the front of this book.